JOSEPH ROTBLAT

A Man of Conscience in the Nuclear Age

To my sons
Jonathan and Martin

MARTIN UNDERWOOD

JOSEPH ROTBLAT

A Man of Conscience in the Nuclear Age

sussex
ACADEMIC
PRESS

BRIGHTON • PORTLAND

2 4 6 8 10 9 7 5 3 1

First published 2009 in Great Britain by
SUSSEX ACADEMIC PRESS
PO Box 139
Eastbourne BN24 9BP

and in the United States of America by
SUSSEX ACADEMIC PRESS
920 NE 58th Ave   Suite 300
Portland, Oregon 97213-3786

British Library Cataloguing in Publication Data
A CIP catalogue record for this book is available from the British Library.

Library of Congress Cataloging-in-Publication Data
Underwood, Martin.
Joseph Rotblat : a man of conscience in the nuclear age / Martin
    Underwood.
p. cm.
Includes bibliographical references and index.
ISBN 978-1-84519-323-2 (p/b : alk. paper)
1. Rotblat, Joseph, 1908–2005. 2. Nuclear physicists—Poland—
Biography. 3. Nuclear physicists—Great Britain—Biography. 4. Nobel
Prize winners—Poland—Biography. 5. Nobel Prize winners—Great
Britain—Biography. 6. Nuclear arms control. 7. Peace. I. Title.
QC774.R67U535 2009
539.7092 aB—dc22
                                                                2009002324

Mixed Sources
Product group from well-managed
forests and other controlled sources
www.fsc.org Cert no. SGS-COC-2482
© 1996 Forest Stewardship Council
FSC

Typeset and designed by SAP, Brighton & Eastbourne
Printed by TJ International, Padstow, Cornwall.
This book is printed on acid-free paper.

Contents

Preface and Acknowledgements

Professor Sir Joseph Rotblat was one of the most distinguished scientists and peace campaigners of the post-Second World War period. He made significant contributions to nuclear physics and worked on the development of the atomic bomb. Yet within a year of joining the Manhattan Project he walked out of it under a cloud: he was suspected of being a Soviet spy. He went on to become one of the world's leading researchers into the biological effects of radiation. His life from the early 1950s until his death in August 2005 was devoted to the abolition of nuclear weapons and to the promotion of peace. For these contributions, together with the Pugwash Conferences on Science and World Affairs, which he helped to establish, he was awarded the Nobel Prize for Peace in 1995. His achievements were ranked with those of Albert Einstein and Bertrand Russell.

The present book is an outline of his influence, his scientific achievements and his tireless pursuit of peace and of the abolition of nuclear weapons. It should appeal to the general reader with an interest in the development of nuclear weapons, in the growth of the anti-nuclear movement and in the peaceful uses of nuclear energy and radioactivity.

I am grateful to the staff of the British Library, and in particular to the Listening Service team, for their assistance during the numerous visits I made there; they made it a joy for me to listen to the tapes of Joseph Rotblat's interviews. I am also grateful to the staff of Fakenham Library, Norfolk, who helped me to obtain books and provided much (and greatly needed) computing and administrative assistance.

I thank Professor Robert Hinde, St John's College, Cambridge, Chairman of the British Pugwash Group; Dr. John Cornwell, Jesus College, Cambridge; Mrs Sally Milne of the British Pugwash Group; and

Professor Norman Kember. They all have read drafts of this book and provided valuable comments and support. Professor Lawrence Badash, University of California, Santa Barbara, has offered me detailed comments on an earlier version, making me clarify a number of issues. I take this opportunity to acknowledge my great debt to him and to convey my thanks.

Cover photograph acknoweldgements (from left to right): Joseph Rotblat as a young man, courtesy of Elspeth G. Bobbs, Santa Fe, and the Los Alamos Study Group, Albuquerque, New Mexico; Bertrand Russell facing a picture of Rotblat taken in 1962, on the occasion of Russell's ninetieth birthday, both pictures courtesy of the Pugwash Conferences on Science and World Affairs; Joseph Rotblat circa 1998, courtesy of British Pugwash. Medals: Manhattan Project commemorative medal; reverse side of Nobel Prize for Peace medal.

Acknowledgements relating to reproducing the text in the Appendixes are presented on page 87.

I am most grateful to the editorial staff at Sussex Academic Press, and in particular to Anthony Grahame, for welcome assistance.

Finally, I wish to thank my wife Mary for reading the drafts of every chapter with a critical eye and for giving me helpful advice on both style and content.

1 | Poland: Early Life and Influences, 1908–1939

Joseph Rotblat was born in Warsaw, Poland, on 4 November 1908. He was one of five surviving children and he describes his early childhood as a very happy one. His three sisters were taught at home and he used to sit in throughout their lessons, which gave him a very early start in education.

Poland was then a divided country. Warsaw was under a tsarist regime and teaching in Polish was banned from schools and universities. Joseph's Jewish father, Zygmunt, built up a nationwide horse-drawn haulage business which specialized in paper transport. Zygmunt owned land and bred horses. Thus Joseph's early years were spent in what was a prosperous household. The family lived in the middle of Warsaw, in a home endowed with a large yard, where the horses were kept along with the carts. Little Joseph had his own pony, played football and enjoyed long walks. The family could afford to take an annual holiday in a chalet outside of Warsaw.

Just before the start of the First World War, the family moved into a newly built flat in a tenement block. However, the builder had run out of money and the flat was not completed; there was no internal bathroom and no lavatory. Clearly the family circumstances were changing by that time – and they altered dramatically at the outbreak of the war, when borders were closed and horses were requisitioned without compensation. The contract with a Finnish company which distributed news print was immediately severed. This turned out to be the death blow to Zygmunt's business. From then on the family endured extreme poverty; they even brewed vodka illegally in order to earn an income. Joseph preserved throughout his entire life memories of starvation from this period. He recounts how hunger drove him to devour even frozen potatoes: he could never bring himself to eat this vegetable again, as it was associated with those terrible experiences.

The end of the war did not improve the family fortunes. Joseph received some formal instruction by attending a vocational school – a 'school for crafts'. His education was practical and involved spending much time in workshops. Later he commented that the teaching there was primitive, with poor mathematics, but at least there was a library. Given the task of cataloguing the books, he started to read voraciously. H. G. Wells and Jules Verne became his favourite authors. He graduated with a diploma after two years, at the age of fourteen, and became straightaway an apprentice electrician.

But Joseph didn't tolerate depending on others, especially when they knew nothing – as he complained about his boss. So he resigned in a matter of months and set up his own business. A budding entrepreneur, he started printing and distributing his own business cards. He began by installing primitive electrical lighting; for at that time lighting was typically provided in the form of gas lamps and candles. But it did not take him long to find a ready market for his skills, since, as he discovered, many people could not even mend a fuse. Moving on to larger projects, he began to install electricity into a series of apartments. This struck him as hard, dirty work: he had to use a hammer and a chisel to put holes through the walls in order to allow the passage of electrical cables. Gradually he became proficient in radio technology and an expert in crystal sets, and yet he barely made ends meet. Still living in poverty, he could not afford the price of a Warsaw tram and walked, or used a horse and cart, to move between jobs.

Joseph Rotblat had an early fascination with science. Initially he was interested in medicine, but then became engrossed in physics. In his day, the normal route into science was through the *Matura*, the entrance qualification for university at the end of the gymnasium; but this was beyond his financial means. However, in January 1929, aged twenty, he found out about evening classes at the Free University of Poland and joined.

These were classes open to Jews and required no *Matura*. Yet the Free University was not really 'free'; he had to make a contribution towards his fees. The premises contained no lecture theatre or special-ist facilities. Experimental physics, for example, was conducted in a building adjacent to the Old Museum. For all these shortcomings, the Free University was a unique institution, set up under occupation, and it received no government support. Typically the staff held socialist views, worked during the day and devoted the evenings to teaching and research, without receiving any salary. Rotblat completed a three-year course and obtained a diploma, but this was not recognized as a degree. He then decided to take the degree course and was one of forty who sat the entrance examination. The exam consisted of two parts. In the general part he was asked to evaluate a book critically and to dis-cuss the effects of the 1773 Education Commission on contemporary education. He had not read the book in question, so he was unable to comment on it, but he collected his thoughts well enough to write cogently on education in general. The specialist part of the exam con-sisted in a paper in mathematics and physics which he found easy. To his relief, he passed.

The Free University had close links with the Miroslaw Kerbbaum Radiological Laboratory of the Polish Scientific Society. Madame Curie, a fellow Pole, served as honorary director. Rotblat went to the Radiological Laboratory as a finalist, to take practical classes. It was there that he came under the spell of Ludwick Wertenstein, whom he described not only as his professor but as his counselor, and who had an immense influence on him at this early stage. Wertenstein had studied with Madame Curie in Paris and spent two years in the Cavendish Laboratory at Cambridge, with Ernest Rutherford and James Chadwick. Rutherford discovered the atomic nucleus; he was awarded the Nobel Prize, knighted and made a life peer. Chadwick discovered the neutron in 1932 and won the Nobel Prize in 1935. Wertenstein himself was a scientist, a scholar, a linguist and a poet. He was also a popularizer of science, writing a weekly newspaper column on the subject. Rotblat commented that, under different circumstances and certainly not under occupation, Wertenstein would surely have risen to the top in Polish culture. What mattered most for Rotblat was Wertenstein's ethical and moral standpoint: it was crucial that his approach to science was human-itarian. Wertenstein instilled in Rotblat the idea that a scientist always bears responsibility for the consequences of his or her work; thus Rotblat came to believe in a 'Hippocratic Oath' whereby scientists would pledge themselves to use their talents for the benefit of humanity. He was always opposed to the view that the discoveries of science are in some sense neutral; according to him, scientists must never be indifferent to what they do and produce.

This belief, arrived at by Rotblat early on under the influence of Wertenstein, was to permeate his future life and work. Robert Hinde has written on this theme (see Braun et al. (eds), 2007), and its importance cannot be overstated. It is clear that it would be a mistake to distinguish Rotblat's views on the responsibility of the scientist from his general notion of responsibility. We clearly have responsibilities towards others in all our activities. However, scientists, he argued, must also take the lead in controlling the uses made of scientific research. The contribution of science to the improvement of human welfare is unquestionable; but it is always difficult to know where a particular line of research might take us, and this can sometimes become problematic. As will be seen later in this book, what appeared at a particular time to be pure research into the interaction of neutrons with certain kinds of matter was to lead to the development of the nuclear bomb. Nevertheless, Rotblat argued that difficulties in anticipating future results should not diminish the scientist's responsibility; the scientist should do everything possible to ensure the good of all.

Rotblat realized that controlling, let alone influencing, the direction of scientific research is not easily achieved. Hence the prime responsibility resides with each scientist as an individual; and this was the thought behind the idea of a 'Hippocratic Oath' for scientists. It is useful to quote the words used by the Student/Young Pugwash movement in the US:

> I promise to work for a better world, where science and technology are used in socially responsible ways. I will not use my education for any purpose intended to harm human beings or the environment. Throughout my career, I will consider the ethical implications of my own work before I take action. While the demands on me may be great, I sign this document because I recognize that individual responsibility is the first step on the path to peace. (Braun et al. (eds), 2007, p. 38)

Hinde and others have pointed out that the intrinsic unpredictability of scientific research makes such an undertaking difficult, if not impossible. On the other hand, the undertaking itself is meaningful only if it has an ethical foundation. Rotblat was of the view that a good grounding in ethics should be part of all scientists' education.

On the other hand, reliance upon the conscience and goodwill of individual scientists will never be sufficient in itself, as individuals are often fallible. Rotblat proposed that a series of ethical committees should be set up to consider research applications; and these bodies would have a human impact, rather like medical ethical committees. Approval from such a body would be a requirement in securing the funding necessary for the pursuit of a particular line of research. In his later years Rotblat spoke out against research being carried out in secret, as is often the case in government and industry. New knowledge, he believed, should be shared. He also raised problems around the commercialization of research, as much university-based science was starting to be funded by commerce. This source of money could influence the direction of research, compromise the ethical issues and increase the secrecy. Along this line of thought, Rotblat came to detest even the patenting of the results of scientific research: in his view knowledge should be freely available.

Of course, the source of secrecy is often the scientists themselves. They impose it because they don't want fellow scientists to be aware of their results until these are published, given that the first publication of a significant result will win its author prizes and accolades. Competition, secrecy and commercialization are all part of science. Views such as the above originated very early in Rotblat's career and, although they became more refined throughout his life, they remained somewhat naïve. He simply wanted to resist certain pressures.

Rotblat started to display his skills as an experimental physicist. At this time there was rivalry between the Paris and the Cambridge groups, especially in the methods used to detect radiation. The Paris group favoured using the piezo effect; the Cambridge group, the scintillation method – and this was also the approach that Rotblat adopted. A third method was the Geiger counter, which detects radiation by counting charged particles produced in the ionization of a gas. Rotblat built his own Geiger counters to detect radiation. He obtained his MA in 1932. In the same year Wertenstein offered him a position at the Free University: not in the Radiological Laboratory, but as Assistant in the

Physics Laboratory. Wertenstein started setting problems for Rotblat. A Polish chemist, Alicia Dorabialska, observed an emission of heat from a number of elements and attributed the phenomenon to the spontaneous emission of neutrons. Wertenstein asked Rotblat to collaborate towards confirming these measurements, but Rotblat could not reproduce them. He was required to build a calorimeter to detect the heat emitted in spontaneous fission but he failed to corroborate Dorabialska's measurements, the heat released being at considerably lower levels than originally reported. Then Rotblat built a much more sensitive differential calorimeter but, again, he failed to detect any emission of heat. In consequence he did not publish the results of this work; he felt he had wasted two years and complained about it.

His job as an electrician was altogether unsatisfactory and very poorly paid, so he gave it up to devote himself to physics at the Free University. He decided to sit for the *Matura* in order to gain access to the University of Warsaw. The examination extended over ten days and covered fifteen subjects. Only three of the initial fifty-five candidates passed, and Rotblat was the only one to pass at the very first attempt. In his judgement, the worst performance he gave in these examinations was in physics; it took him fifteen minutes to write the paper.

During his period in Warsaw Rotblat made major discoveries. His work on inelastic neutron collisions is of great importance. It was believed until then that neutrons underwent elastic collisions; in other words they would not lose energy, behaving in the manner of billiard balls. However, Rotblat demonstrated that neutrons experienced inelastic reactions and could lose considerable amounts of energy when they collided with a nucleus. In his experiments, in order to scatter neutrons, he used a one-kilogram block of gold borrowed from the Mint. Apparently he would collect it every morning and return it on the evening of the same day – and this went on for some months. (One could well wonder whether the London Mint would still be so trusting of an experimental physicist nowadays.)

Rotblat took pride in the fact that he used a very weak neutron source, namely 30 mg of radium in solution. The radon produced was mixed with beryllium powder to produce neutrons. By contrast, the eminent physicist Enrico Fermi, who worked in Italy and was to win the Nobel Prize for Physics, used 1 gm of radium and discovered a large number of radioactive materials by bombarding the elements with neutrons. Soon after the discovery of the neutron, Fermi realized that this was a powerful method to create artificial radioactive materials. True, such materials had already been found by bombarding the nucleus with charged particles; nevertheless the new method was an important step forward, as the neutrons were not repelled by electrostatic forces. Despite the comparative weakness of his neutron source, Rotblat discovered some radioactive isotopes missed by Fermi, including ^{60}Co (an isotope of cobalt), which was to prove invaluable as a gamma-ray source in radio-therapy.

Rotblat went on to hold the position of Research Fellow in the Radiological Laboratory of the Scientific Society of Warsaw and became assistant director of the Atomic Physics Institute of the Free University of Poland in 1937. Elsewhere other neutron sources were being developed; they were produced by using accelerated charged particles, for instance the cyclotron and the electrostatic generators known as the Cockcroft–Walton sets. He decided to build a 600 kV machine in the Free University, but there was little money available and the machine failed.

During the same period, in 1937, Rotblat married a Polish student of literature, Tola Gryn, whom he had met in 1930; their relationship, although short-lived, was to prove pivotal to his life. He wrote his doctoral dissertation on inelastic neutron scattering in 1936/37 and was awarded the degree by the University of Warsaw in 1938. He only regretted that his father had not lived long enough to see him receive his doctorate.

While still in Warsaw, but with Wertenstein encouraging him to work abroad, Rotblat became aware of the work of Otto Hahn and Fritz Strassmann, who bombarded uranium (U) with 'slow' neutrons and discovered the presence of a lighter material, barium. The two communicated their results to Lise Meitner and Otto Frisch, who then realized that the uranium nucleus had split or fissioned. There are two forms of uranium in a natural state: ^{238}U and the far less abundant ^{235}U (which is less than 1 per cent). Niels Bohr, who was one of the founding fathers of quantum physics, developed a model of how physics worked across the atom and nucleus; and he suggested that ^{235}U was the element responsible for fission. Neutrons should be emitted in the process of fissioning. This observation was corroborated in other laboratories. Rotblat, who had started working on uranium too and repeated these experiments, was able to show that in the process of fissioning the neutrons emitted were in larger numbers than the ones absorbed. He wrote a paper in Polish on the subject for the journal *Nature*; but, while Wertenstein was translating it into English, he found to his distress that Frederic Joliet-Curie had come up with similar measurements and published them first. Early in 1939, Rotblat envisaged that a large number of fissions could occur and that, if this happened in a short enough period of time, considerable amounts of energy would be released. Thus Rotblat calculated that this process could occur in less than a microsecond and then its consequence would be an explosion. The idea of an atomic bomb came to his mind in February 1939.

During the same year, through Polish connections originating with Marie Curie, Rotblat was invited to study in Paris. He was also invited to work with James Chadwick, who had moved to Liverpool University. Chadwick was building a cyclotron in order to study fundamental nuclear reactions and, as Rotblat wanted to build a similar machine in Warsaw, he decided to join him in Liverpool. At this stage he commented on the fact that, having finished his studies, he could not get an academic post in Poland.

2 | Liverpool University, 1939–1944

Rotblat travelled to England in 1939. He went alone, since he could not afford to support Tola there: the Polish authorities had awarded him a fellowship to the value of just £120 per annum. He travelled by train and stopped in Belgium, where he had a paternal cousin – the only cousin who was to survive the war. It just so happened that, his cousin's daughter needed a blood transfusion and, as Rotblat was of the same blood type (0), he gave her blood.

He arrived to Liverpool on 18 April, coming from Paris via London, after ten days of journeying. He was immediately shocked by the slums, which he thought to be worse than in Poland. He found accommodation with other students at 13 Abercrombie Square, within five minutes' walk of the university. The cost of his room, all meals included, was £117 and 6 pence per annum, which left him with a very small surplus, of under £3, for all other expenses during the year. On arrival he became aware that his English was poor, and he had massive problems understanding the Liverpool accent. His less than perfect grasp of the language could produce solecisms; once, for instance, when penning a letter of thanks after a weekend in the country, he wrote: 'thank you for being so hostile to me' (BLSA). What is more, his grasp of social mores did not come much to the rescue: he had read *The Forsythe Saga* and P. G. Wodehouse in Polish and thought that that was how the English behaved.

Rotblat was surprised to discover the poor state of the facilities at Liverpool, which were of a lower standard than those in Warsaw; for instance the physics teaching laboratory lacked an AC electricity supply (that is, an alternating current supply of the kind used now in all our domestic supplies). The department was divided into two, one part being devoted to teaching and the other to research. The latter was where Chadwick was building the cyclotron. Chadwick surrounded himself by young staff, whereas the older staff were confined to teaching. Rotblat described Chadwick as a shy, introspective person – a man of few words. He was invited to Chadwick's house for Sunday tea on his first weekend in Liverpool and was made to feel very welcome by Chadwick's wife. He became fond of their twin daughters. According to his testimony later on, he was the only member of Chadwick's department to be invited to his home. This was an early indication of Chadwick's regard for Rotblat.

However, Rotblat himself was in despair about his poor grasp of English, although on the other hand he was not taking lessons to improve it. On one occasion, upon attending a lecture in physics, he complained to Chadwick that he had not been able to understand any of it. Chadwick responded that he did not understand it either. Such was Rotblat's plight that he considered leaving for Paris; but, having written to his wife about it, he received advice from her to remain in England. Her attitude – with hindsight, one might call it prescience – probably saved his life. Later on Rotblat became active in the Polish community.

Right from the start, Chadwick assigned Rotblat some tasks connected with the measurement of short-lived radio-nuclides. One of Rotblat's earliest experiments at the University of Liverpool consisted in the application of two Geiger radiation detectors – an experiment designed to measure radioactive lifetimes between 1/10 second and 1/10 of a microsecond. This demonstrated fully his skills as an experimental physicist. The measurement was to become part of his PhD thesis and made a significant contribution to the subject.

Impressed with Rotblat's work, Chadwick awarded him the Oliver Lodge Fellowship, which brought his income to £240 per annum. Now, with sufficient funds, Rotblat returned to Warsaw in the summer of 1939, with the intention of bringing his wife Tola to England. The story of this journey is narrated in interviews. Here is one anecdote from them: he had managed to buy a pineapple and planned to take it home to Poland, where this fruit was a rarity. However, that was a time of IRA bombing in London; and, as 'pineapple' could mean 'bomb' in the jargon of those days, he thought better of it.

He planned to return to England in late August 1939, accompanied by his wife. Unfortunately Tola developed appendicitis, so he went back to Liverpool alone, in the expectation that she would follow; for she already had the necessary papers. However, Germany invaded Poland on 1 September 1939, one day after his return to Liverpool. War was declared on 3 September and Tola was stranded. Rotblat made increasingly desperate attempts to bring her out of Poland through Belgium, Denmark and Italy, but these attempts failed as borders closed across Europe. Ultimately, Tola died in the Majdanek concentration camp. British Intelligence knew about this in 1941, but Rotblat did not find out until 1945, from a 'phone call he received from his sister. This event affected him deeply for the rest of his life. He was to say, much later, that he felt he could have done more to save her.

After the outbreak of war, the stipend he received from Poland stopped, so that he failed to receive the final £30 payment for the year. In these circumstances he decided to visit the Polish Embassy. He hitch-hiked to London with no more than 7 shillings and 6 pence in his pocket – only to find chaos.

His personal relationship with Chadwick continued to be good; there were regular house visits, fishing trips and holidays taken together. As a mark of his regard for Rotblat, Chadwick appointed him to a temporary lectureship in nuclear physics. This spurred him on to improve his English rapidly in order to be able to deliver undergraduate lectures.

As we have seen, Rotblat was aware of fission. In the summer of 1939 he started to think more about its military uses. At first, his poor mastery of English prevented him from raising these issues at Liverpool, but on his return to Poland in August he submitted to Wertenstein, for discussion, his calculations concerning the feasibility of a bomb. Wertenstein had not considered such matters before. He listened to Rotblat's nascent thoughts on deterrence – which included the view that one had to develop nuclear weapons in order to deter Hitler. He offered no other advice than to follow one's conscience; he, Wertenstein, would not develop such weapons. On his return Rotblat felt compelled to raise these matters in Liverpool too. Now, at the outbreak of war, his colleagues there were being diverted to work on radar. He presented his ideas on the feasibility of a uranium-fuelled bomb directly to Chadwick. Chadwick's initial reaction was silence; then he urged Rotblat to start immediate work on inelastic neutron scattering.

Rotblat was given two assistants to facilitate this work: an Australian and a Quaker. The latter was sent to Liverpool to teach physics because he was a conscientious objector. Hence Rotblat was forbidden to reveal to his assistants the purpose of their experiments; he described them simply as 'pure' physics, but he certainly was ridden with disquiet and guilt about this deception.

Rotblat's primary reason for working with Chadwick in Liverpool was to conduct experiments on the cyclotron, which was becoming operational just when he arrived. This 37-inch cyclotron accelerated charged particles – for instance it accelerated protons to an energy of over 8 MeV and deuterons to an energy of up to 4.1 MeV – and, if particles thus accelerated collided with other nuclei, nuclear reactions could occur. (The MeV is a measure of energy equivalent to the energy acquired by an electron accelerated to 1 million volts.) Later applications included the production of radioactive isotopes and studies of radioactive decay. However, from the outbreak of war until the end of 1943, work on the bomb consumed almost all of the time available for the cyclotron.

Chadwick encouraged Rotblat to make measurements on the energy of the neutrons generated through fission and on the proportion of neutrons which were absorbed by other nuclei without producing fission. Then Rotblat went on to work on ^{235}U and made fundamental measurements on the cross-section of ^{235}U for fission neutrons, the scattering cross-section for neutrons and the energy spectrum of fission neutrons. These experiments demonstrated that the nuclear bomb was feasible; but it would take massive technological and industrial effort to produce sufficient quantities of the ^{235}U isotope required to manufacture a bomb.

One must stress here Rotblat's ingenuity and brilliance as an experimentalist. Together with Cecil Powell of Bristol University (who went on to win the Nobel Prize for Physics), he pioneered the use of sensitive photographic emulsion to detect neutrons and to measure the associated energy and angular distribution of emissions. In that emulsion, the neutrons collide with protons which recoil and leave tracks of silver grains, the length of which can be measured by using a microscope. The work performed was incorporated in Rotblat's Liverpool PhD thesis. He also undertook fundamental work on spontaneous fission in uranium and showed that the number of neutrons emitted in that process was about the same as the number of neutrons emitted under induced fission.

In 1940 a committee known as the Maud Committee was set up to consider the prospects of making a uranium-fuelled bomb. This came about largely as a result of the work of the physicists Otto Frisch – an experimentalist of Jewish Viennese extraction who worked with Niels Bohr in Denmark and with Chadwick at Liverpool – and Rudolf Peierls, a German-born mathematical physicist who was working at Birmingham University. They followed Niels Bohr's suggestion that ^{235}U was responsible for fission and they showed that the amount of material required to make a bomb was of the order of kilos – and not a tonne, as had been estimated. Both Frisch and Peierls were classed as enemy aliens and were not initially in a position of being able to take part in the deliberations of the committee. This was absurd, since the very foundation of the Maud Committee was a consequence of their work; so they were eventually allowed to serve on a technical sub-committee. Interestingly, Rotblat was classed as a friendly alien, and in this capacity he was not allowed to leave his lodgings from sunset to sunrise, to ride a bike or to own a map!

Frisch and Peierls visited Chadwick in Liverpool and discussed the production of uranium hexafluoride (the only gaseous form of uranium known to be stable), which could be processed to enhance the content of ^{235}U. Shortly after this meeting, Frisch decided that the place for him to continue his work was Liverpool, since Liverpool had an intense neutron source, the cyclotron, and was not dedicated to work on radar. Chadwick offered him a job.

Liverpool was subject to air attack and Rotblat took up fire watching at the university every second night, having been given permission to break the conditions of his curfew. He saw an incendiary bomb fall on No 16 Abercrombie Street; an explosive bomb fell on the Physics Department. Fortunately the cyclotron remained unscathed, as it was housed in the basement.

Once he found himself back in England after his visit to Poland, Rotblat was wrestling more and more with his conscience during those early days in Liverpool. He asked himself the question: 'What should I do? Should I begin to work on it?' (meaning of course the bomb). Central to Rotblat's view was that he considered himself to be a 'pure scientist'; it was not his job to work on weapons of mass destruction. However, he was well aware that other scientists, and in particular German ones, did not necessarily share his convictions. Put simply, the community of scientists was aware that, if Hitler had the bomb, he would win the war. When Poland was overrun, Rotblat made the decision to work on the bomb. His belief was that the allied scientists needed to do this in order to make it possible for the bomb *not* to be used. In other words the reasoning goes: if it is possible for Hitler to have the bomb, then the only way we can prevent him from using it (against us) would be by us having it too (without using it). This is the theory of deterrence.

Many mathematicians and physicists had been diverted to work on radar because such work was given priority at the outbreak of war. One leading group was that of Mark Oliphant of Birmingham University, who was developing the key radar component. He visited the US in 1940 to discuss radar problems and, to the consternation of some, he openly discussed work on a uranium-based fission bomb. The Americans promptly dispatched two physicists to visit Liverpool and to meet Chadwick's group. The US became increasingly interested in work produced in the UK. The Americans then set up a project to build a uranium-fuelled fission bomb, which was code-named 'the Manhattan Project'.

3 | The Manhattan Project, 1944–1945

It was now clear that the need to separate out usable amounts of ^{235}U was paramount. A pilot plant was set up in North Wales but came to a standstill. At the outset of the war there was little contact with the Americans on nuclear war-related work, but it was known that they had built a large, 60-inch cyclotron; at the same time Enrico Fermi had built a reactor. Fermi had done fundamental work on neutrons in Rome, but when he was awarded the Nobel Prize in 1938 he did not return to Italy; he started work at Columbia University in New York.

The Los Alamos Laboratory in New Mexico was set up in 1943. This was to be the centre of the work on the Manhattan project. Other laboratories were also involved – for instance the Oak Ridge Laboratory, which concentrated on isotope separation. As has been pointed out by Lawrence Badash (1995), even before the laboratory buildings were complete, apparatus was arriving from American universities; Harvard sent a particle accelerator. There were number of key initial objectives, including the experimental confirmation that a chain reaction – that is, the very rapid build-up in the release of neutrons – did occur as it was predicted. The speed of these reactions is crucial: sufficient energy must be released before the material designed to make up the bomb is simply blown apart. There was also a need to determine the sub-critical mass – in other words, a mass just below the amount needed to sustain a chain reaction. Also, the final shape of the material needed to be determined. As there are 'stray' neutrons around us due to the bombardment of the atmosphere by energetic particles from deep space – particles known as cosmic rays – it was necessary to have the fissionable material in a sub-critical mass. The method used was that of dividing the material into two parts and then bringing them together at great speed, to initiate an explosion. This was done by placing ^{235}U effectively in a gun barrel and by using conventional explosives to shoot into another piece, thus creating a nuclear explosion.

Following a summit meeting in 1943 between the US president and Churchill, it was decided that the British should join the US effort to produce the bomb. The British team, led by Chadwick, included Otto Frisch and the theoretical physicist Klaus Fuchs, who was to be exposed later as a Soviet spy. The team left England in late 1943, but without Rotblat. The Americans had insisted that only British citizens could join the project, and Rotblat was a Polish citizen. He had resisted taking British nationality, as he intended to return to Poland after the war. However, two weeks later, he was instructed to come out to America, and he left by boat for New York. During his stay in New York he took the opportunity to purchase the short-wave radio which was to feed him with information at Los Alamos. He then proceeded to the Pentagon to be interviewed by General Groves, the head of the Manhattan Project. General Groves gave him permission to join the project and to retain his Polish nationality – a privilege accorded to no one else. Next, Rotblat traveled by train to Santa Fe and finally by car to Los Alamos, some twenty miles further on.

The US Army had set up the Los Alamos School for Boys. This building was converted into a laboratory which, by the end of the war, had grown into a real 'town' of some 7,000 scientists and engineers with their families. Rotblat initially stayed with the Chadwicks and then was allocated two rooms in the 'Big House', as it was known – a building made out of tree trunks – having Frisch as a neighbour. Frisch and Rotblat were friends from Liverpool, and the latter was to confess that the initiative for any social life outside the laboratory came from Rotblat. Frisch was also an accomplished pianist and performed at a concert for a group of Polish soldiers organized by Rotblat in Liverpool. He played Chopin's grand *Polonaise* to a rapturous reception.

Rotblat was instantly struck by the scenery, the Rocky mountains being only some thirty miles away. Another pleasant surprise was his pay, which made him feel rich. Assigned as he was to the Cyclotron Division, he was amazed by his fellow scientists: he could sit down to lunch with six Nobel Prize winners. The collection of talent at Los Alamos was astonishing. The scientists and engineers were taken from enterprises such as the development of the radar and were strongly motivated by the desire to develop weapons such as the bomb before Hitler may have a chance to do it. This was very much Rotblat's driving force too.

The personnel at Los Alamos consisted indeed in some of the world's leading scientists. The director was the theoretical physicist Robert Oppenheimer, who had studied in Germany in the 1920s with some of the founding fathers of quantum theory and of the so-called 'new physics' – the field that was to prove very successful in descriptions of the atom, and in particular of the nucleus. Oppenheimer recruited the best physicists, chemists and engineers and thought of his group as a community, not just a collection of scientists. Badash tells us that

> the streets were muddy when it rained, the water supply became overtaxed, and the residents were pressed to create a town council to battle their army overlords on many urban problems. This common experience, plus the intensity of their work, created a strong feeling of camaraderie, and Los Alamos 'alumni' often looked back to the period 1943–45 as the high point of their lives. (Badash 1995, p. 43)

This was not true for Joseph Rotblat, as I hope to demonstrate later. Other leading physicists engaged in the project included Hans Bethe, who developed the theoretical description of nuclear processes occurring in stars; Edward Teller, whom I will present later as the 'father' of the hydrogen bomb (or H-bomb); the very young Richard Feymann, whose texts are now known to many undergraduate physicists; and the remarkable Victor Weisskopf. Enrico Fermi arrived in 1944.

The facilities were magnificent and Rotblat was able to order any equipment he wanted. He recounts how he once sent a 'chit' for a barber's chair, just to see whether he could get away with it; and the chair arrived promptly four days later. On General Groves' subsequent visit Rotblat told him that, working twenty-four hours a day as they did, they hardly had any time to visit a barber!

Rotblat was happy at the beginning. He believed that it would take a considerable amount of time to make the bomb; the war might be over by then, and hence there would be no need for a bomb in the first place. However, very early on he came to have ambivalent feelings about his involvement in the project. It is thought that he made no significant contribution to the development of the bomb; he even complained of having nothing to do. The fact is that he soon became uneasy about the nature of his work. Perhaps the most important factor conducive to this was his growing realization that the purpose of the bomb was not quite the one he had envisaged. During a visit to Los Alamos, General Groves declared at a dinner party that the primary reason for developing a bomb was to defeat Stalin and to subdue the Soviets. Rotblat was appalled, since the Soviet Union was our ally. Moreover, he objected to the censorship of his letters, which he considered highly intrusive. Rotblat's ambivalence about the project deepened when he was able to conclude that, given the enormous scientific, technological and financial effort involved in producing a bomb, Germany simply did not have the resources for it.

There was a crucial incident concerning his friend Elspeth Grant which hardened his views about the whole project and about his engagement with it. Elspeth Grant was a law student from Liverpool whom he had met before 1944. She suffered from a genetically inherited hearing problem. Her father was American, and she was allowed to move to the US on medical grounds. She planned to visit Santa Fe and wanted Rotblat to write to her. When she finally moved there Rotblat went to see her with Chadwick's permission, but not with the approval of the Intelligence services. This prompted some, notably in the Los Alamos security, to imagine that maybe he had not been totally discreet and talked to Elspeth about his work. The US Intelligence service started to regard him with a good deal of suspicion; in all probability he was considered a spy.

In the meantime, Niels Bohr joined the Manhattan Project and became a close friend. The two of them listened to the news each morning on Rotblat's short-wave radio. Like him, Bohr too wanted to prevent an arms race with the Soviets and suggested collaboration under international supervision and control. Bohr even managed to convince Roosevelt of the wisdom of this plan; but Churchill remained unconvinced.

Here is a statement which captures Rotblat's state of mind at the time:

I was in Los Alamos for less than a year. Well, I came in the beginning of 1944, and left by the end of 1944. As soon as I came to Los Alamos, I realized that my fear about the Germans making the bomb was ungrounded, because I could see the enormous effort which was required by the American[s], with all their resources practically intact, intact by the war – everything that you wanted was put into the effort. Even so, I could see that it's still far away, and that by that time the war in Europe was showing that Hitler is going to be defeated, and I could see that probably the bomb won't be ready; even that Hitler wouldn't have it in any case. Therefore I could see this from the beginning, that my being there, in the light of the reason why I came to work on it, was not really justified. But nevertheless, I could not be sure that the Germans would not find a shortcut maybe and they could still make the bomb. Therefore I kept on working together with the other people, although I was very unhappy about having to work on it. But as soon as I learned, towards the end of 1944, that the Germans have abandoned the project, in fact a long time before, I decided that my presence there was no longer justified, and I resigned and I went back to England. (Transcript of interview from BLSA)

In 1985, in a seminal paper for the *Bulletin of Atomic Scientists* entitled 'Leaving the bomb project' (Appendix 1), Rotblat declared that working on the Manhattan Project had been a traumatic experience, and one which endured throughout his future life. It is not often given, and certainly not to anyone, to participate in the birth of a new era, he observes. He goes on to say that there was growing evidence that the war in Europe would be over before the completion of the bomb project, which made his participation in the latter pointless. If it took the US such a long time to develop the bomb, then his fear of the Germans getting there first was groundless. In fact it became evident towards the end of 1945 that the Germans had abandoned their efforts in this direction; hence the whole purpose of his being at Los Alamos had vanished. There Rotblat put very clearly the view that the notion of using his knowledge to effect mass destruction was totally abhorrent to him.

Rotblat asked himself why other scientists did not make the same decision: why did they not leave? For some of them, scientific curiosity was paramount. They wanted to know whether the theoretical predictions would turn out to be true. Others believed that the work should continue, on the grounds that many American lives would be saved if the weapon was used to bring about a rapid end to the war with Japan. Some agreed that the work should have ceased when it became clear that Germany had abandoned work, but they feared that entertaining this view or acting on it could harm their future career.

Rotblat left Los Alamos in December 1944. He traveled via Washington, where the Chadwicks had transferred by that time, and then by troop-ship from New York to Cardiff. He left all his books, papers and notes with Chadwick's military assistant, who was to put them in boxes and ship them to England. The papers disappeared and have never been seen since. Rotblat arrived in Cardiff in January 1945, convinced that he had been watched by the US Intelligence on his journey back. This was very upsetting for him.

The time spent in Los Alamos was perhaps the pivotal intellectual experience of Rotblat's life, while the loss of Tola can be seen as his central emotional experience. But there was more to it. Chadwick was highly concerned about the implications of the fact that a participant from Britain – Rotblat – was the first one to leave the Manhattan Project; and indeed the Americans regarded him as a security risk. The consequences were far reaching. To begin with, he was denied an entry visa for the States for many years.

4 | Under Suspicion

Rotblat had problems from the outset. He was considered a security risk, together with Rudolf Peierls, Otto Frisch and others. Although he had retained his Polish citizenship with special permission from General Groves, he was put under constant surveillance by Los Alamos security. (As for his citizenship, when Poland was overrun by the Soviets, he realized that he could not return there, so as things turned out he was naturalized as a British subject.)

As I have already mentioned, the contact with Elspeth Grant caused him considerable difficulties and fuelled suspicions that he might be a spy. She had moved to Santa Fe, which was a bus journey from Los Alamos. Rotblat visited her once, then returned to offer condolences after the death of her brother. When he started taking flying lessons on Sundays in a Tiger Moth near Santa Fe, he visited Elspeth on a regular basis. Their conversations were overheard by – so it seems – a Hispanic house janitor with a poor command of English. Elspeth eventually obtained her FBI file under the Freedom of Information Act but found it almost entirely blacked out, so she was unable to discover the identity of the person who had briefed against them. Rotblat himself considered Santa Fe to be full of spies.

In Rotblat's obituary penned by Brian Cathcart for the *Independent* of 2 September 2005, it was stated:

on visits to nearby Santa Fe, he had befriended a young English woman who was in New Mexico for treatment for a hearing problem. Evidently Rotblat had been more open about his work than he should have been, and she had been equally indiscreet, discussing him with a friend. This friend, a Santa Fe woman with a gift for embroidery, convinced herself and the security agents that the Pole was up to no good.

These remarks prompted a response from Joyce Bazire, a former lecturer in English Language at Liverpool University and a long-standing friend (see Rowlands and Attwood (eds), 2006); and his reply elicited in turn another letter, this time from Elspeth Grant to Joyce Bazire. In this letter Elspeth writes:

> Joe never said anything at all about what he was doing at Los Alamos, nor would I have asked nor understood anything about it anyway. However, what is not mentioned is that what we did discuss was Russia, politics and the war. We were both socialists then with some admiration for Russia and ignorant of the atrocities committed by Stalin, and then Russia was saving England however reluctantly, by making an heroic stand against Hitler. We had the European view of communism, and did not regard it as with the same horror as Americans. I think this was why my friend and surrogate mother made up lies about me and passed them on to an Army Intelligence officer whom she knew. (Ibid., p. 129)

She adds, by way of justification, that 'she was a pious Catholic and, to her, godless communism was worse than fascism, which was at least Christian'. Concerning the Hispanic janitor, Elspeth wrote: 'I do not believe this. My house was bugged and I think that's where the garbled information came from' (Rowlands and Attwood (eds), 2006, p. 133; also on BLSA).

When Rotblat told Chadwick of his wish to leave the Manhattan Project, Chadwick reported it to the Intelligence chief. As Rotblat tells us, he was shown

> a thick dossier on me with highly incriminating evidence. It boiled down to me being a spy: I had arranged with a contact in Santa Fe to return to England, and then be flown to and parachuted onto the part of Poland held by the Soviets, in order to give them the secrets of the atom bomb. (Appendix 1)

However, Rotblat was able to show that some of the times and dates included in the dossier were fabrications. The chief of Intelligence accepted Rotblat's rebuttal and promised to destroy the dossier. Then Rotblat saw the head of the British Intelligence, who made the same promise, assuring him that the dossier would be destroyed. Nevertheless, Rotblat was able to establish the continued existence of the dossier as late as the 1990s.

Rotblat was allowed to see Elspeth one more time in Santa Fe, and he assumed that the meeting was observed by US Intelligence agents. After a trip to England in 1950, she returned home to discover that the CIA had visited the place several times. She was subjected to gruelling interrogations about her visits and informed that she was a communist spy who had leaked information to the enemy. The CIA wanted to know everything that Rotblat had ever said.

After these events Rotblat continued to be treated with great suspicion by the American Intelligence community. In 1950 he was invited to a nuclear physics conference in Chicago, but his visa application was rejected.

5 | Return to Liverpool, 1945–1950

When he returned to Liverpool, Rotblat was put in charge of nuclear physics there, as Chadwick stayed on in America. He was very much involved in reviving nuclear physics in the country; he was member of a newly formed Nuclear Committee which included Patrick Blackett from Imperial College, a scientist whom he described as the 'big shot' of nuclear physics. He was Chair of the Accelerator Panel, and under his control a design was produced for a cyclotron at the Atomic Energy Authority Harwell Laboratory. He also proposed the building of a much bigger and higher energy accelerator at Liverpool – a synchro-cyclotron. This was a machine requiring a 156-inch magnet which, he believed, was the largest that could be produced at the time. Its cost, in 1946, was £330,000. When he went before the Funding Panel, it so happened that a scientist he knew, who was there just ahead of him, was asking for small amounts of money to purchase some microscopes and was turned down; but his request for the sum of £330,000, which was huge at the time, was instantly approved. It was then he realized that decisions of this magnitude were made elsewhere, by higher authorities.

There was a problem: this accelerator could not be housed within the Physics Department. It was decided to house it in the crypt of the proposed new Roman Catholic Cathedral. The crypt had already been built, but it was deconsecrated in preparation for hosting the accelerator. However, the new cathedral was considered to be an inappropriately ostentatious project in austere post-war Britain, and the Roman Catholic Church decided to cancel it. There is a wonderful coda to the whole story. Ratblat went on holiday to Italy in 1947 and wanted to take a tour of the catacombs in Rome. He arrived late, yet the guide still took him round; and Rotblat was astonished to discover during their conversation that this Italian knew about the plans to install an accelerator in the crypt of the proposed Liverpool Cathedral.

Rotblat was also Chair of the Photo-Emulsion Panel. During the war he had collaborated with Cecil Powell on using photographic emulsion to detect neutrons. More sensitive emulsions were needed to detect lighter particles and competing contracts were given to Kodak and Ilford, both of whom came up with emulsions of similar sensitivity. These emulsions were used to study the energy levels of nuclei. Powell discovered a new nuclear particle, the pi-meson, which brought him the Nobel Prize for Physics.

Rotblat was appalled by the use of the atomic bomb on Hiroshima (of which he heard on the radio) and subsequently on Nagasaki. Partly in reaction to the horrors of the atomic bomb, he became more interested in the medical uses of nuclear radiation. Liverpool had a long history of involvement in medical physics, starting from the early use of X-rays by Oliver Lodge in 1896. James Chadwick came to Liverpool to build a cyclotron because he was given little support in Cambridge to do it. Chadwick had established from the outset that the use of the machine for the production of radioactive isotopes for medical applications was important, as was its use for fundamental studies in nuclear physics. Investigations into the radioactive isotopes of calcium were undertaken in 1940, and the cyclotron was used to make isotopes for an Oxford neurosurgeon in 1943. In 1947, Chadwick published in the *Lancet* an important paper which showed that two isotopes, namely those of iodine and phosphorus, had found practical applications. He also suggested the use of radioactive trace elements in the investigation of chemical reactions in the body.

Rotblat was at the vanguard of the medical applications of radioactivity, being made Chadwick's deputy on his return to Liverpool and then head of department after Chadwick's departure for Cambridge in 1948. He collaborated with George Ansell of the Department of Medicine and pioneered the use of ^{131}I (produced from a reactor at Harwell) in the treatment of thyroid problems. In particular, he could differentiate between the presence of goitre – an enlargement of the thyroid gland – and that of a tumour. A goitre preferentially takes up iodine, and if a radioactive form of iodine is used it is possible to locate the disease using radiation detected outside the body. The isotope ^{131}I decays through the emission of beta and gamma rays, the gamma rays leaving the body and being detectable by a Geiger counter. A novel detector was constructed. It had a collimator added to the Geiger counter in order to measure accurately the intensity of the gamma rays produced. Rotblat's paper concerning the detection of goitre was considered so important that it has been reprinted by the *British Journal of Radiography* in its history series.

In 1949 Rotblat summarized the medical applications of radioactive tracers around a discussion of three principal techniques:

- the sample technique;
- the in-situ method;
- the radio-autograph.

In each of these three cases, a safe dose of a radioactive isotope is administered and its activity is measured as a function of time. In the sample technique, biopsies or urine and blood samples are taken at regular intervals and the activity is measured in this way. The in-situ method relies on the measurement of radiation – typically, gamma radiation – outside the body. The radio-autographic technique makes use of photographic emulsions: samples are placed directly on the emulsion and the activity is measured by this procedure.

Rotblat's research concentrated increasingly on the medical applications of radiation and radio-isotopes. This interest culminated in his application for a post which he obtained: the Chair of Physics as applied to medicine at St Bartholomew's Medical College.

6 | St Bartholomew's Medical College, 1950–1976

By 1949, Rotblat felt that he had done enough work in the application of physics to medicine to look for a full-time job in this area. During that year a chair became available at St Bartholomew's Medical College, which was part of the University of London. The physicist Leo Szilard had worked with the department at St Batholomew's while Rotblat was in Warsaw, but had never visited it. Now Rotblat applied for the chair and was appointed professor of physics at St Bartholomew's Hospital Medical College, a title he retained until his retirement in1976. However, the appointment was not without problems and he could not take up his post until 1950.

The interviews were held in July/August 1949, in the expectation that the successful candidate would start in October 1949. Twelve people had been shortlisted. Rotblat had a brief interview, then heard nothing. He telephoned the Registrar, who informed him that there were problems. In general, medical physicists had good relationships with clinicians. However, when Rotblat put his name forward for a professorship in physics (applied to medicine), the Bart's medical establishment rejected him. One of the problems was the question of why someone of his standing in the field of nuclear physics should want to come and teach first-year medical undergraduates – which was a key part of the job; another was his desire to spend money on research. Rotblat himself believed that the reluctance to appoint him might have been a consequence of his left-wing political views, given that Bart's was seen as a somewhat conservative institution. It was clear that he was already one of the leading figures in the field; at the interview he was recognized by another candidate, who remarked: 'We might as well all go home now.' The University of London intervened in the dispute and told Bart's that they would either 'have him, or no one'.

He accepted the post in September 1949 but had to stay in Liverpool for one more term, to work his notice and help in the appointment of his new successor – for the one already appointed, who was one of Fermi's colleagues, had defected to the Soviet Union only a week before taking up Rotblat's position. Once he moved to London, Rotblat's first task was to find some where to live, and not just for himself but also for his mother, his brother, his sister in law and their daughter – all of whom had joined him in Liverpool. When he visited London in 1939 on the way from Liverpool to Warsaw, he had stayed in Hampstead and walked up Primrose Hill. This made such an impression on him that his heart was now set on living in that part of London. He was helped in this by a friend from Warsaw, a chemical engineer and linguist, who had started a business there as an agent importing scientific instruments. When the war broke out, this man and his wife moved to the eastern parts of Poland. The region fell under Soviet occupation and the two were sent to separate Gulags. After some years, the Poles were allowed to leave if they served in the Soviet Army. Rotblat's friend was eventually reunited with his wife and found his way to England. He traced Rotblat through the editor of *Nature* and resumed their friendship. Now he alerted Rotblat to a house advertised in *Dalton's Weekly* which was in the right location – 8 Asmara Road – and could accommodate his extended family. The owner wanted £4,500, but Rotblat could borrow no more than £4,000. To his disappointment the house was sold to someone else; but after looking elsewhere for some time he found that his original choice was back on the market. The previous purchasers had withdrawn and lost a deposit of £500. Rotblat then offered his available £4,000. This time his offer was accepted and the family moved in December 1949 to 8 Asmara Road, where Rotblat lived until his death in 2005.

Within the medical college his primary job was to teach physics to first-year MB undergraduates. Often these students came from school with no background in physics and he found that it was more difficult to teach them than students at a higher level. However, he very much enjoyed the challenge and described himself as a born teacher. He was always diligent in his duties and arranged his research work so as to be able always to deliver his lectures. He took pride over the fact that, in twenty-six years of giving three lectures a week, he never missed one. There are few eminent scientists who could make such a claim.

In 1957 there was a nuclear reactor accident at Sellafield; it was known as Winscale and resulted in the release of radiation to the atmosphere. This incident spurred Rotblat towards promoting the development of an MSc in Radiation Physics, together with Professor Roberts of the Middlesex Hospital. Once this was done, he set up an MSc in Radiation Biology with Professor Patricia Lindop, who was to become one of his most important collaborators.

At that time there was a physics department both in the medical college and in the hospital. This reflected the uses of radiation in diagnosis and therapy. There was also the post of chief physicist to the hospital, which had been occupied by Frank Hopwood, Rotblat's predecessor at St Bart's. During the war Hopwood moved to Cambridge, and it was expected that his deputy, George Innes, would step into his place. However, Rotblat was summoned before the Board of Governors of St Bart's and offered the post of chief physicist to the hospital. The hospital was apparently keen to appoint – in his own words – a 'great scientist', whereas Innes was an engineer. Rotblat describes his relationship with Innes as somewhat fractious.

What characterized Rotblat's work while he was in these two posts was the fact that he established links across all disciplines in hospital and college. He set up a Department of Nuclear Medicine in the hospital, using radioactive techniques both to diagnose and to treat cancers. He also created a Department of Nuclear Electronics and introduced ultrasound to the hospital. He was proud to point out that there were about 120 staff in the hospital when he retired.

Rotblat's immediate problem was to develop radio-therapy. Before 1950, cancer radio-therapy was carried out using gamma-rays from sources of high voltage X-rays. Bart's was in possession of an X-ray machine with the (then) very high rating of 1MV. The problem, however, was that, in order to treat deep-seated tumours, the doses of radiation required caused considerable damage to the skin and to the tissue between it and the tumour. Improvements were made by using the gamma-rays produced by ^{60}Co, an isotope of Cobalt which could be generated in reactors. However, far better prospects were in view from the use of linear accelerators.

When Rotblat arrived at Bart's in 1950, approval had already been given to purchase a Mullard Bimodal Linear Accelerator with both X-ray and electron facilities, operating at 15 MeV. This machine, known as a LINAC, was originally installed in the medical college in Charter House Square and was used for research rather than for treating patients. Rotblat also found out that the college had the money for undertaking research: one million pounds was available. The LINAC had the capability of delivering an electron beam at full current (Rowlands and Attwood (eds), 2006). The team developed a quadrant monitoring system and a 'knock-on' dosimeter system to centre the beam and measure the output. A pulse selection unit was developed which could control the number of pulses of the electrons delivered and the space between them. A horizontal 14 MeV electron beam could be extracted giving a dose of 0.4 or 1cGy per pulse, with a pulse width of 1.3 micro-seconds. (This is the Gray, the unit of absorbed radiation dose, defined as being equivalent to a dose of 1 Joule per kilo-gram.)

Rotblat was quite open about his involvement in the development of this accelerator. He described himself as a showman and the accelerator, initially, as his 'toy'. He has some stories to tell about it. One is about him using the LINAC to irradiate some wine in order to mature it and then inviting the Lord Mayor of London to a tasting. When the wine was offered, it was found to be rancid, as it had been overexposed to radiation. Another anecdote is about the opening of the accelerator: Rotblat had organized this to be performed by the Duke of Gloucester from a distant lecture theatre; but the then Dean of Middlesex Hospital Medical School walked in, went straight to the machine and triggered it off. Rotblat suggests, mischieviously, that this was done deliberately to spoil the party.

With the LINAC available for research in the medical college (later on it was transferred to the hospital to treat patients), a most successful collaboration developed between Rotblat and Patricia Lindop. Those were the days of the creation of the National Health Service. The hospital was reluctant to join it. Bart's was an altogether conservative institu-tion, which did not admit women as medical students. Patricia Lindop was one of the first. She went ahead to do research, working with the professor of physiology, and wanted to use radio-isotopes. This led to her collaboration with Rotblat.

For Rotblat, one of the key issues was to understand the mechanisms underlying the effects of exposure to radiation. To this end he used mice, who were exposed to radiation. His work on mice, published in 1961, indicated that the medium life-span of a mouse was reduced by about 5 per cent if a dose of 1 Gy was delivered to them. There also appeared to be a linear response to dosage, and there was no threshold; in other words, at zero dose no effect was evident, and the effect increased linearly with dosage from that point on. The conclusion was that the shortening of life was a consequence of the increased incidence of diseases; and some diseases (for instance leukaemia) contributed to this more than others. Further studies using mice were undertaken, but there was an outbreak of disease among the mice population and most had to be destroyed, which left the experiment a failure. However, some information was salvaged which indicated the protective effect of hypoxia at the time of irradiation. This line of enquiry was pursued in the investigation of radiation, which was used to treat tumours in mice. It turned out that the effects of radiation on these tumours were greater when a dose was delivered in two fractions than when the same dose was delivered at once. The fact was attributed to an increase in the oxygenation of the tumour following the first dose of radiation. This observation led to the treatment of patients under hyperbaric conditions. Research to assess the effects of radiation was later carried out on cells grown in culture, because this procedure dispensed with the need to care for thousands of mice. The fundamental difference was that cell experiments do not allow for investigations into blood-flow related effects.

In the 1970s, a new 15 MeV Vickers Research LINAC was installed, now in the medical college: so this was a dedicated research machine, which did not compete for time with the patients' need of treatment. However, this machine was not a great success. Norman Kember, who succeeded Rotblat as head of the Academic Department and subsequently became a professor, wrote that 'the apparatus . . . never lived up to its specification' and goes on to say 'in spite of the expenditure of large research funds and some few research students, the apparatus produced just one research publication-great men are allowed to make great mistakes' (Rowlands and Attwood (eds), 2006, p. 165). Kember goes on to say that 'the academic Department of Physics was kept separate from the Hospital Department of Physics. This was a policy that led, in part, to the eventual closure of the Academic Department . . . I was not in

Joe's league as a scientist or administrator' – of whom he comments: 'he was a hard act to follow'.

Rotblat was to go on to serve as the vice-dean of the Faculty of Science in the University of London and as treasurer to St Bartholomew's Medical College. He was proud of being chief editor of the journal *Physics in Medicine and Biology*, in which capacity he served for thirty years. He was president of the Hospital Physicists Association and president of the Institute of Radiology, which was a rare honour for someone who was not medically qualified.

7 Politics: Rotblat's Growth into a Public Figure

On 6 August 1945, America exploded a nuclear bomb over the Japanese city of Hiroshima. Rotblat heard this piece of news on the BBC and, by his own admission, was devastated. He had left the Manhattan Project by then, and he hoped that the bomb would not work. Failing that, he hoped that it would be used as a demonstration weapon only: once its explosive might was revealed, it would bring an end to the war. He felt very strongly that scientists should be at the vanguard of efforts to prevent the development and proliferation of nuclear weapons. A key change occurred in Rotblat's thinking at this time. He realized that the argument to develop nuclear weapons that permitted him to work on them, that is, the argument for deterrence, was false. It would not have worked with Hitler, because Hitler would have used such weapons in spite of any consequences. Rotblat's own reasoning in favour of working on nuclear weapons was invalid. He proposed what looks like a naïve idea: that there should be a moratorium on research related to nuclear weapons. He talked to his colleagues in Liverpool, knowing this to be a drastic plan; nevertheless it seems that it had a warm reception.

This encouraged him to explore the idea with others too. He went to the universities of Oxford, London and Cambridge to talk to physicists, but by his own admission he received only a mixed response. Interestingly for him, the harshest opposition to his proposals came from left-wing physicists, including Blackett from Imperial College and Powell, with whom he worked closely during the war. Their point was that the US would have a monopoly over nuclear research and would dictate matters until the Soviets developed nuclear weapons too.

In 1946 Rotblat took the lead in setting up the Atomic Scientists Association (ASA) in order to stimulate public debate. ASA included many of the leading scientists of the day. It adopted a non-political agenda, with the aim of educating the public on the peaceful uses of radioactivity and on issues related to nuclear power. A project called 'the atom train' was conceived. As part of it, Rotblat went to the Ministry of Supply in the government to ask for a loan for a travelling exhibition which was designed to demonstrate many aspects of radioactivity, including its peaceful applications. The exhibition consisted of two converted railway carriages which contained a series of exhibits. It would cost one shilling to get in, so they would recover the costs. Together, Rotblat and Peierls wrote a guide-book for the exhibition which was priced at six pence and sold 53,000 copies.

Chadwick opened the atom train in 1947; over 150,000 people attended as the train travelled to Chester, Blackpool, Scotland and Wales. The exhibition closed in 1948. UNESCO then wanted it, as they had repaid a part of the initial loan. So the exhibition went abroad, to Europe and then to Beirut, where a UNESCO World Congress was being held. Concerning the latter travel, Rotblat records an accident. The voltage was different in Beirut; a transformer was needed to operate the equipment, but it blew. So the exhibition went ahead with one exhibit coming on after another, sequentially and somewhat tediously, rather than simultaneously. Next, the atom train travelled to Egypt and Iraq.

The aim of this exhibition was to

help you understand the facts about atomic energy. Everyone knows that this new power can be used for destruction; much less is known as yet of its possibilities for good. Some have exaggerated ideas of what atomic energy can do for us, or think it will give cheap power to-morrow. Others do not believe it will ever be very useful because nothing very useful has come of it yet. One can get a balanced view only by understanding a little of what is behind it.

After passing through the exhibition you will not be an expert on the subject. You will not understand all the details of the working of an atomic plant. You probably also do not understand all the details of the working of your radio set or watch. Yet you do not regard watches or radio sets as mysteries; you have got used to them, and you have heard something of the principles that make them work. If we have given you a little of the same feeling for atoms and nuclei, regarding them as things that really exist and whose effect you have seen, we shall be well pleased.

If what you have seen makes you think about these questions, and has made you look for books and other information on the subject, then the effort that has gone into the preparation of this exhibition will have been well worth while. November, 1947. (Rowlands and Attwood (eds), 2006, p. 283)

Rotblat made two interesting remarks about the atom train. First, Prime Minister Attlee did not approve of the exhibition, as he did not want discussions about the peaceful uses of nuclear power or the arrival of an exhibition marking 'atomic energy week'; he wanted the bomb. Secondly, the profits from the guide-book kept the ASA running for some years.

Rotblat was brought very much into the public eye when the Americans began the development of the thermo-nuclear or hydrogen bomb (the so-called H-bomb). A leading theoretical physicist at Los Alamos was Edward Teller, whom Rotblat knew – their offices had been adjacent. He describes him a rather reserved man, and the reason for his reserve became clear. It turned out that Teller had applied his considerable skills to the next question: What would be the consequences of the fusion of light nuclei such as those of hydrogen and deuterium (an isotope of hydrogen)? Fusion is a process opposite to fission: in fusion the nucleus is blown together rather than pulled apart (as it is in fission). Physics shows that a great deal of energy would be released if the temperature of a mixture of hydrogen/deuterium could be raised sufficiently highly for the necessary reaction to occur. This could be achieved by using the fission bomb as the trigger.

Another important player entered the stage at this point: this was Klaus Fuchs, who had been at Los Alamos too. After the war Fuchs became head of the Theory Division at the Atomic Energy Establishment at Harwell. All the research conducted at Los Alamos was reviewed in order to determine what could be de-classified and released into the public domain. A Joint US/Canadian/UK Committee was formed. Fuchs had access to all the papers, including the blueprint of the Nagasaki bomb, and he supplied the Soviets with information. The US security services cracked the code he was using to do so. He was charged and, pleading guilty, he was sentenced to fourteen years, out of which served nine. Rotblat was full of contempt for Fuchs; he used to point out that other spies had been executed. Fuchs had an easy time of it in prison too, running the library, and was returned to East Germany, where he received no less than a professorship. Rotblat met him a few years later, at a conference in the Soviet Union, and remarked that he had remained an ardent communist. The Fuchs affair was to have wider ramifications. Rudolf Peierls, with whom Fuchs had been associated, came under very strong suspicion, which persisted for many years, in a widening climate of general mistrust.

The Soviets successfully conducted the test of a bomb in 1949. The US authorities were stunned, not being aware of the consequences of the leaking of information. It is said the General Groves believed that it would take them twenty years to develop a bomb. This prompted the US to develop the hydrogen bomb under the leadership of Edward Teller. Rotblat took a particular interest in the testing of America's second hydrogen bomb at the Bikini Atoll on 1 March 1954; this was known as the 'Bravo Test'. Next month, in April, the BBC organized a *Panorama* programme to discuss the hydrogen bomb. Rotblat, the Archbishop of York and the leading philosopher Bertrand Russell were invited. Rotblat was to explain the physics of the hydrogen bomb, and the others were to discuss its moral implications. This was his first meeting with Bertrand Russell, and it was to be the start of a remarkable relationship.

Rotblat explained that the fusion process driven by the fission trigger would result in about one thousand times the heat and blast yield, with no increase in the release of radiation. However, this did not accord with what came to light after an accident involving 'Lucky Dragon', a Japanese fishing boat whose crew of twenty-three was fishing eighty-five miles to the east of Bikini Atoll. They all became contaminated when the wind changed direction after the initial blast.

A Japanese physicist whom Rotblat met at a conference gave him information on the dosage of radiation which he analysed. Jack Broag, a long-standing friend who was also his colleague at the time, recalls:

Joe invited me down into his office and told me he had calculated that the Bikini bomb must be a 3-stage device. Its large yield identified it as a fusion bomb, triggered by a central fission core, but the fallout must have come from the fission of a very large quantity of ^{238}U. Ergo, the outer casing of the bomb must have been made of ^{238}U, which would fission when struck by the fast neutrons from the fusion explosion. It was the so-called 'dirty bomb'. (Rowlands and Attwood (eds), 2006, p. 45)]

Rotblat drafted a note for *Nature* about all this; but first he consulted Sir John Cockcroft, now chairman of the United Kingdom Atomic Energy Authority, who advised delay. Here we can see the shadow of the Fuchs affair. Cockcroft's point was that this was not long after the scandal of the news that Fuch was a spy. Mistrust and suspicion were rife, so that releasing this kind of information could be seen as divulging 'secrets'. There was a general reluctance to upset US authorities. What particularly distressed Rotblat was the briefings, which suggested that those exposed to radiation after the test had received a dose which was no larger than they would have received from a typical X-ray. He knew that this was at best misleading, if not downright false. However, soon afterwards Ralph Lapp, an America physicist, published similar conclusions, so Rotblat went ahead with the publication of his paper.

The movement against nuclear testing started to grow. Bertrand Russell decided that the public should be warned of the perils of nuclear weapons and on 23 December 1954 he made a radio broadcast, highlighting some of the issues. Rotblat's paper, which denounced the Bravo Test, was soon picked up by the press and in a short time Rotblat became, in his own words, 'a great celebrity'.

Early in 1955 Rotblat was asked by the BBC to appear both on radio and on television to discuss nuclear weapons and weapons testing. These programmes were subsequently cancelled. Rotblat firmly believed that this was a result of government pressure and that then Prime Minister Winston Churchill had intervened personally. His exposure of the nature of the Bravo Test bomb was seen by some as an unnecessary whistle-blowing; but Bertrand Russell regarded it as an important piece of detective work. Russell was firmly of the view that scientists needed to be galvanized and to take the lead, revealing to the public the perils of nuclear weapons and their testing.

Early in 1955 Russell wrote to Albert Einstein, the most prominent scientist of the day, to express the opinion that some form of statement was needed from him. He drafted a letter and sent this to Einstein for signing, together with his message. On 18 April, on a flight from Rome to Paris, Russell learned that Albert Einstein had died. Yet on arrival to Paris he discovered that the letter had been forwarded and signed: this was one of the final acts of Einstein's life. Russell then tried to gather some Nobel Prize winners, including those from the Soviet and eastern block countries, and make them sign too. However, as there were very few Soviet Nobel Prize winners, he relaxed the requirement of their participation. There was one Pole among the eleven signatories: the physicist Leopold Infield. The youngest signatory was Rotblat himself, whom Russell asked to participate on the ground that he, too, would receive the Nobel Prize one day. This document is known as 'the Russell–Einstein Manifesto'. It was decided to make it public, and Keith Harris from the *Observer*, who had written about Rotblat after the *Panorama* interview, organized a press conference for a launch at Caxton Hall in London. There was considerable interest in this event; the largest room was booked – for 9 July 1955. The week before the press conference Rotblat was on holiday in Ireland, at Bray near Dublin. There the local police called at his cottage (which had no telephone) to take him immediately to the police station, where he received a telephone call from Russell. Russell was calling to ask him to chair the press conference, reasoning that Rotblat would be able to answer any technical questions asked.

On the Saturday of the press conference the room was full of journalists. The meeting opened with Rotblat introducing Bertrand Russell, who read the statement and was greeted with great applause. The appeal of the statement was partly due to the powerful rhetoric of expressions such as 'as human beings to human beings', 'members of the human race' and the like. Yet Rotblat was not entirely happy because Russell failed to mention the other signatories of the manifesto. Also, he incorrectly referred to Rotblat as being from Liverpool University instead of St Bartholomew's Medical College (where Rotblat already had a chair, as we have seen).

This manifesto was a crucial document (see Appendix 2). It was signed by ten scientists together with Bertrand Russell. All were, or were to become, Nobel Laureates (NLs). They were: Max Born, Germany

(NL Physics 1954); Percy Bridgman, USA (NL Physics 1946); Albert Einstein, Germany (NL Physics 1921); Leopold Infeld, Poland; Frederick Joliot-Curie, France (NL Chemistry 1935); Herman Muller, USA (NL Physiology or Medicine 1946); Linus Pauling, USA (NL Chemistry 1954); Cecil Powell, UK (NL Physics 1950); Joseph Rotblat, UK; Bertrand Russell, UK (NL Literature 1950); and Hideki Yukawa, Japan (NL Physics 1949). As one can see, Rotblat was one of two among the signatories not to have won a Nobel Prize at the time; his Nobel Prize for Peace was to come in 1995.

Here is a telling sample of the tenor of the manifesto:

> [I]n a tragic situation which confronts humanity, we feel that scientists should assemble in conference to appraise the perils that have arisen as a result of the development of weapons of mass destruction, and to discuss a resolution in the spirit of the appended draft. We are speaking on this occasion, not as members of this or that nation, continent, or creed, but as human beings, members of the species Man, whose continued existence is in doubt. (Appendix 2)

The manifesto goes on to say that we have to learn to think in a new way; we should not ask what is required to achieve a military victory for our nation, province and so on, but what steps can be taken to prevent a military engagement that would be disastrous to all parties. The manifesto points out that neither the general public nor many of those in authority have fully realized the consequences of nuclear war. It is not just a matter of major cities such as New York or Moscow being destroyed, terrible as that would be; nuclear weapons can spread destruction over far wider areas. When a bomb explodes, radioactive particles enter the atmosphere, fall and reach the earth as dust or rain, spreading over large distances. As a result of this process, a war with the hydrogen bomb could bring about the end of the human race. The manifesto asks: '[S]hall we put an end to the human race; or shall mankind renounce war? People will not face this alternative because it is so difficult to abolish war.' The signatories recognized that the abolition of war would mean limitations on the power and influence of sovereign states, but they warned that the alternative we face is possible total destruction. The manifesto ends with a call to

invite this Congress, and through it the scientists of the world and
the general public, to subscribe to the following resolution. In view
of the fact that in any future world war nuclear weapons will be
certainly employed, and that such weapons threaten the existence
of mankind, we urge the Governments of the World to realize, and
to acknowledge publicly, their purpose cannot be furthered by a
world war, and we urge them, consequently, to find peaceful means
for the settlement of matters of dispute between them.

Bertrand Russell was contacted by a Canadian steel, coal and railway
billionaire, Cyrus Eaton, who lived in a village of Nova Scotia called
Pugwash and offered to pay the expenses for those who wanted to meet
and discuss these issues. This was initially thought to be a hoax, as the
name 'Pugwash' was associated with children's stories at that time.
Russell did not reply. He approached the Greek shipping magnate
Aristotle Onnasis, asking him to host a meeting after the declaration of
the manifesto. A conference was organized in India, Cecil Powell making
the necessary arrangements to meet in Delhi. This meeting was notable
in that four scientists arrived from the Soviet Union. Although Rotblat
helped to prepare the agenda for the meeting, he could not himself
attend.

This meeting occurred at about the same time as the First
International Conference on the Peaceful Uses of Nuclear Weapons,
whose associated exhibition was a means by which US companies could
sell nuclear reactor technology. This helped scientists to become more
aware of the peaceful uses of nuclear energy. However, the development
of nuclear reactors for the production of electricity also allowed the
production of the substance plutonium, which could undergo fission
just like uranium and hence offered the basis for bomb-making. It
became increasingly clearer at this time that controls were needed in
order to limit the production of plutonium. This is how the idea of an
International Atomic Energy Authority was formed; and such a body
was subsequently established.

Rotblat became more of a public figure when he was asked to make
programmes for the BBC on the peaceful uses of nuclear energy, ten years
after Hiroshima. As part of this he went to Geneva to interview scientists, and Niels Bohr happened to be there. Not surprisingly, the BBC
was keen to interview him. Bohr had a speech impediment which made

him difficult to follow, so his presentation was read by someone else. This was high-profile television exposure for Rotblat. He made three programmes. The first two were concerned with nuclear power generation and the associated costs and safety implications; the third was concerned with the medical applications of radioactivity. Rotblat demonstrated the presence of radioactivity using a Geiger counter and was accused of being something of a showman. These imputations echoed some of the criticisms surrounding the opening of the LINAC at St Bartholomew's Medical College. Rotblat's programmes raised the question of how much one should inform the press and general public, given that distortions and exaggerations of the underlying scientific discourse can easily occur. In the aftermath of debates on the consequences of testing nuclear weapons and the subsequent fallout, there was growing talk about the birth of deformed babies. Rotblat gave an interview to the *Sunday Chronicle* addressing this topic but, to his mind, the interview was grossly distorted afterwards. He wrote to *The Times* about his problems with the press and prepared to sue the *Sunday Chronicle* (which folded prior to any action on his part).

Rotblat tried to organize a meeting of the ASA in 1956, but the political climate was not conducive. This was the time of the Suez crisis and of the Hungarian uprising, which ended in the Soviet invasion of Hungary. In 1957 more nuclear tests occurred and the ASA set up a Committee on Radiation Hazards, of which Rotblat was president. The committee concluded that nuclear testing could cause cancers and genetic defects, especially from strontium. A statement was made which was picked up by the press and Rotblat was denounced in the House of Lords by Lord Cherwell, who believed in the threshold theory – that is, the theory that small amounts of exposure to radioactivity were not harmful but that the harmful effects would only begin after a certain level of exposure. The political climate was one where this was convenient to believe, so as to not alarm the public about the harmful effects of nuclear weapons testing. Rotblat considered this to be a dangerous viewpoint; as we have already seen, Rotblat subsequently demonstrated in his mouse experiments at St Bart's (which were not published until the early 1960s) that this was not the case. The vice-president of the ASA warned that he would resign if he was not consulted in the future on announcements made to the press. For Rotblat, this marked the beginning of the end of the organization.

8 | The Pugwash Conferences

In 1957 Rotblat decided to organize a conference and approached Cyrus Eaton to see whether his offer was still open. It was. Eaton promised to cover all the traveling expenses of the participants and to provide accommodation and hospitality for a conference to be held in July of that year. (The early years of Pugwash are vividly described by Rotblat in *Pugwash. The First Ten Years*.) Eaton saw it as an opportunity for scholars and educators 'to relax, exchange views, sharpen their own thinking and design formulae for us to live in this brand new world'. He had set up an educational institution which, as it turned out, allowed him to set off these expenses against tax. Bertrand Russell was not able to attend but he sent a message. It was important to Rotblat that scientists should participate; but some feared that the conference was politically motivated. Out of the twenty-two participants, fifteen were physicists, two were chemists, four were biologists and one was a lawyer. Attendees were from the US, the Soviet Union, the UK, China, France, Poland, Australia, Japan, Austria and Canada. Rotblat flew to Montreal, then to New Brunswick on Eaton's private jet, and from there proceeded to Pugwash by car.

Cecil Powell was the Chairman, with Rotblat as Secretary. Leo Szlilard was there and, in Rotblat's own words, took over the meeting. The agenda consisted of three main headings:

- radioactive fallout: this section concerned the hazards from war and testing, and was chaired by Rotblat

- how to stop the arms race getting out of control
- the social responsibilities of the scientist.

Rotblat was of the view that at that first conference the greatest progress was made on radiation hazards. Not much was known at the time concerning the biological effects of radiation and the consequences of nuclear testing and nuclear war. This meeting was the start of a dialogue between scientists from the West and from Soviet Union.

The discussions were largely of a scientific nature; this was probably the reason why there was at least some level of agreement. The conference highlighted the social responsibilities of the scientist. It also demonstrated that scientists have a common purpose which transcends national boundaries. Despite political differences, they could discuss the issues and problems surrounding nuclear weapons.

At the end of the meeting, a statement was produced (see Appendix 3). The statement acknowledged that, although two years had elapsed since the publication of the Russell–Einstein Manifesto, the dangers remained. In fact, the stockpiles of weapons had increased and new nations had joined the ones which possessed nuclear armament. Considering the hazards arising from the testing of nuclear weapons the committee concluded that, compared with other hazards facing mankind, these were small. It was recognized, however, that certain geographical areas may be subjected to much higher risks; in consequence, close attention should be paid to the possibility of danger. A principal effect of radioactive fallout is due to strontium, which causes leukaemia and bone cancer. The committee estimated that the nuclear tests conducted up until then would result in an increase of about 1 per cent over the natural incidence of leukaemia and bone cancer throughout the coming decade. The long-term genetic effects were estimated to be on a similar scale. The committee compared the effects of exposure to radiation from sources such as medical X-rays and nuclear power and concluded that fallout from nuclear tests represented only a small increase over normally occurring phenomena; but the effects could be localized, some areas of the world experiencing a higher than average proportion of effects from fallout.

The conference considered the possible consequences of a nuclear war. The unquestionable conclusion was that an unrestricted nuclear war would represent a disaster of unprecedented magnitude. The radiological hazards would be thousands of times greater than the hazards arising from the testing of nuclear weapons and associated fallout. Hundreds of millions of people would be killed by the blast, heat and radiation produced. If a 'dirty bomb' were employed, then large areas would be made uninhabitable for long periods of time and hundreds of millions would die from direct radiation, injury, delayed effects, and – in succeeding generations – from genetic defects. Then the committee considered the issue of arms control against the background of the conclusions outlined above. It pointed out that the objective of all the nations must be the abolition of war (and even of the threat of war) from the life of mankind. War must be, not simply regulated by restricting the number of nuclear weapons, but altogether eliminated. This objective calls for the lessening of tensions between nations; the ending of the arms race; effective arms control systems; and the suspension of nuclear bomb tests.

In considering the role of scientists, the committee concluded that it is their prime responsibility to do everything in their power, outside their professional work, to prevent war and to help to establish a permanent and universal peace. Scientists from all countries can contribute to this end insofar as they share common beliefs. Here are some of them:

1 With the penetration of science into the world of atomic nuclei, humanity has entered a new epoch.

2 The development of science and technology has paramount importance for the future of all mankind. This imposes upon scientists the obligation to be more actively concerned with matters of public policy, and upon political leaders the duty to take fully into account the scientific and technological facts.

3 As a consequence of human mastery over nuclear forces, a war can now cause immeasurable damage to mankind.

4 If the achievements of science are rationally employed, they could enormously increase the wellbeing of humans.

5 Scientific and technological progress is irreversible. With humanity basing much of its technological progress on the manipulation of nuclear forces, it is of paramount importance that war be made permanently and universally impossible.

6 In the past, nations have often resorted to force in the quest for

natural resources and fruits of labour. These methods must now be replaced by a common effort to create wealth for all.

7 The security of mankind demands that no section of it shall have the capacity to destroy the other. The developments of science and technology tend to break down barriers between nations and, in effect, to unify mankind.

8 The need of parts of mankind to cooperate in the growth of the total sum of human knowledge and wealth, despite ideological and other differences which may divide them, is permanent and not a matter of temporary 'coexistence' of different political or economic systems.

9 In the education of youth, tradition tends to place the emphasis on the separate ideals of single nations, and these ideals include the glorification of war. The atomic age urgently requires a modification of these traditions. Without abandoning loyalty to national heritage or to fundamental principles of different societies, education must emphasise the permanent community of the interests of mankind in peace and cooperation, irrespective of national boundaries and differences in economic or political systems.

10 Science has a well proven tradition of international cooperation. We hope that this cooperation can be strengthened and extended into other fields of human endeavour.

11 Science develops most effectively when it is free from interference from any dogma imposed from the outside, and when it is permitted to question all postulates, including her own. Without this freedom of scientific thought and without the freedom to exchange information and ideas, full utilization of the constructive possibilities of science will not be possible.

Rotblat's view was that the statement from the First Pugwash Conference made some impact on society, but not quite as much as was hoped. The statement was widely reprinted. The Academy of Sciences of the Soviet Union adopted it; and it received much publicity in China. In Rotblat's view the response was slow in the West, but the message of the conference was acknowledged by many scientists.

It must be stressed that those who attended the Pugwash conferences did so as individuals, not as representatives of any organization, and the meetings were private. The participants would meet as scientists and discuss political issues; but they considered themselves to be a collection of scholars, and the skills of lawyers and economists would be called upon as the political influence of Pugwash grew.

The First Conference was planned as a one off event, yet the committee agreed to meet again and consider ways to halt the arms race. An agenda developed and it was decided to carry on with the Pugwash Conferences. Cyrus Eaton publicized the meeting.

Rotblat was invited to Japan by Hidekei Yukawa, Nobel Award winning physicist and signatory of the manifesto; and on this occasion he visited Hiroshima. Once there, he went to a hospital which treated some of the survivors of the bomb experiment. The US authorities had not allowed the Japanese to collect their own statistics on radiation exposure and its consequences. Also, they had destroyed a cyclotron. The radiation dose received in various parts of Hiroshima and in the surrounding areas was extremely difficult to determine. Then it was proposed to collect photographic film from various shops around Hiroshima and to use them in order to gain a rough idea of radiation dose levels – a novel idea. However, the films were confiscated by American military forces, and the US set up the Atomic Bomb Commission with the express purpose of determining radiation exposure and dose levels. Leukaemias started to occur, just as Rotblat had predicted.

In 1957, five members of the Continuing Committee from the first meeting in Pugwash met for the first time at St Bartholomew's Medical College in Rotblat's office; Szlilard was very much in evidence and Bertrand Russell took the chair. This meeting centred around the question of future conferences and their type. Russell very much favoured an open format, with a view to engaging the wider public in the issues debated at the conference. But this proposal was vetoed. It was agreed that there would be annual scientific meetings designed to address the general problems facing the world at large, as well as smaller workshops. Cyrus Eaton was contacted and he agreed to finance subsequent conferences. Europe was suggested as a venue, but Pugwash was chosen for the IInd Conference. Yet the event took place eventually in Quebec, since Pugwash was covered in snow.

Rotblat admits that a great deal of his time, from 1957 down to his retirement in 1975, was taken up with Pugwash organizational work. It was agreed that the UK should take the lead in organizing subsequent conferences. Bertrand Russell was appointed chairman and Rotblat was designated secretary general a couple of years later. There was no office and no funding. Rotblat used his secretary out of office hours. The official address of the conference was his own home address: 8 Asmara Road.

The IInd Pugwash Conference comprised twenty-two scientists, predominantly from the US, Soviet Union and UK. The Continuing Committee was aware that what was needed were participants with expertise in nuclear disarmament. The scientific lead was taken by Patricia Lindop. The topics discussed included the dangers of the current world situation; ways of eliminating nuclear weapons; and ways of reducing the inevitable tension surrounding the possession of nuclear weapons. For Rotblat, the principal value of the IInd Conference was in the fact that the exchange of views between the participants was completely open.

The third meeting, in Vienna, allowed for wider public access; but the press was excluded. The main items on the agenda were: the consequences of nuclear war; aspects of disarmament; the ramifications of living in a scientific age; and the responsibilities of scientists. A session was devoted to future plans and the form that the conferences should take. It was agreed that the most important function of the meetings was to create opportunities for scientists from a variety of nations to meet and to confront openly the problems facing the world, especially the ones presented by the existence of nuclear weapons. There was general agreement that the conferences were of value and should continue. The Continuing Committee was to determine the agenda for the next meeting, the efforts being concentrated on 'topics which are directly related to the easing of international tensions, the establishment of systems of mutual security, the elimination of war as an instrument of national policy, nuclear control and disarmament, and the role of scientists in creating a peaceful and abundant world'.

There followed 'The Vienna Declaration' (Appendix 4). In summary, this powerful document is divided into seven parts. Part 1, 'Necessity to end wars', states:

[A]lthough the nations may agree to eliminate nuclear weapons and other weapons of mass destruction from the arsenals of the world, the knowledge of how to produce such weapons can never be destroyed. They remain for all time a potential threat to mankind. In any future major war, each belligerent will feel not only free but compelled to undertake immediate production of nuclear weapons;

for no state, when at war, can be sure that such steps are not being taken by the enemy. We believe that, in such a situation, a major industrial power would require less than one year to begin accumulating weapons. From then on, the only restraint against their employment in war would be agreements not to use them, which were concluded in times of peace . . . the decisive power of nuclear weapons, however, would make the temptation to use them almost irresistible, particularly to leaders that are facing defeat. (Appendix 4)

Part 2, 'Requirements for ending the arms race', argues:

[T]he armaments race is the result of distrust between states; it also contributes to this distrust. Any step that mitigates the arms race, and leads to even small reductions in armaments and armed forces, on an equitable basis and subject to necessary control, is therefore desirable. . . . We recognize that the accumulation of large stocks of nuclear weapons has made a completely reliable system of controls for far-reaching nuclear disarmaments extremely difficult, perhaps impossible. For this disarmament to become possible, nations may have to depend, to a practical degree of technical verification, on a combination of political agreements, of successful international security arrangements, and of experience of successful co-trust, which does not now exist, and an assurance that nations recognize the mutual political advantages of avoiding suspicion. (Appendix 4)

Part 3, 'What war would mean', points out that

the local fallout from the use of 'dirty bombs' would cause the death of a large part of the population in the country attacked. Following their explosion in large numbers (each explosion equivalent to that of millions of tons of ordinary chemical explosives), radioactive fallout would be distributed, not only over the territory to which they were delivered, but, in varying intensity, over the rest of the earth's surface. Many millions of deaths would be produced, not only in belligerent but also in non-belligerent countries, by the acute effects of radiation and that even tactical weapons now have a large radius of action; cities and towns are commonly closely associated with centres of supply and transportation. We, therefore, believe that a 'restricted' war would lead, despite attempted limitation of targets, to widespread devastation of the territory in which it took place, and to the destruction of most of its population. (Appendix 4)

Part 4,'Hazards of bomb tests', reaches the conclusion that

bomb tests produce a definite hazard and they will claim a signifi-cant number in present and following generations. Though the magnitude of the genetic damage appears to be relatively small compared with that produced by natural causes, the incidence of leukaemias and bone cancer due to the radioactivity from the test explosions may, in the estimate in the UN Committee, add signifi-cantly to the natural incidence of the disease. . . . [I]t goes without saying that the biological damage from a war, in which many nuclear bombs would be used, would be incomparably larger than that from tests; the main immediate problem before mankind is thus the establishment of conditions that would eliminate war. (Appendix 4)

Part 5, 'Science and international cooperation', focuses on the signifi-cance of scientists:

[W]e have an important contribution to make towards establishing trust and cooperation between nations. Science is, by long tradi-tion, an international undertaking. Scientists with different national allegiances easily find a common basis of understanding; they use the same concepts and the same methods; they work towards common intellectual goals, despite differences in philo-sophical, economic, or political views. The rapidly growing importance of science on the affairs of mankind increases the importance of the community of understanding. . . . [W]e call for an increase in the unrestricted flow of scientific information among nations, and for a wide exchange of scientists. We believe that nations which build their national security on secrecy of scientific developments sacrifice the interests of peace, and of the progress of science, for temporary advantages. It is our belief that science can best serve mankind if it is free from interferences by any dog-mas imposed from outside, and if it exercises its right to question all postulates, including its own. (Appendix 4)

Part 6, 'Technology in the service of peace', stresses again the importance of the scientist:

> As scientists, we are deeply aware of the great change in the condi-
> tion of mankind which has been brought about by the modern
> development and application of science. Given peace, mankind
> stands at the beginning of a great scientific age. Science can provide
> mankind with an ever increasing understanding of the forces of
> nature and the means of harnessing them. This will bring about a
> great increase in the well-being, health, and prosperity of all men.
> (Appendix 4)

Finally, Part 7, 'The responsibility of scientists', reiterates the primary
position of scientists in Pugwash:

> We believe it to be the responsibility of scientists in all countries to
> contribute to the education of the peoples by spreading amongst
> them a wide understanding of the dangers and potentialities
> offered by the unprecedented growth of science. We appeal to our
> colleagues everywhere to contribute to this effort, both through
> enlightenment of adult populations, and through education of
> coming generations. In particular, education should stress improve-
> ments of all forms of human relations and should eliminate any
> glorification of war and violence. (Appendix 4)

The IVth Conference was in Baden, Austria, but was not funded in any
way by Cyrus Eaton. This conference stressed that Pugwash meetings
were private, but not secret. Privacy was crucial for the success and
progress made at the Pugwash Conferences.

The Vth Conference in 1959 was funded by Eaton, who paid the traveling expenses of most of the participants and provided hospitality at
Pugwash. Of interest at this conference was especially the discussion of
the threat posed by chemical and biological weapons.

The VIth conference was held in Moscow in 1960 and adopted the
Vienna Declaration of 1958. The VIIth and VIIIth conferences were held
in Stowe, Vermont and discussed international cooperation in science,
disarmament and world security.

By 1962 the Pugwash Conferences had been in existence for five years, and the Continuing Committee felt that it was appropriate to review past activities and to plan for the future. It was believed that decisions towards achieving these aims and towards the election of a new Continuing Committee should be made by a wide group of scientists, and all the participants in past conferences were invited. It was decided that the Continuing Committee should have representatives from the UK, the US and the Soviet Union and the chairman should be Bertrand Russell.

In 1962 Pugwash held joint meetings in Cambridge and London – the IXth and Xth conferences respectively. The Cambridge Conference preceded the London one and concerned itself with disarmament problems. The meeting divided into working groups which discussed the following topics:

1 problems of reduction and elimination under international control of weapons of mass destruction and of their means of delivery;
2 problems of balanced reduction and elimination of conventional armaments;
3 political and technical measures for contributing to the lessening of international tensions (including the nuclear test ban and consideration of activities in space);
4 problems of security in a disarmed world;
5 economic aspects of disarmament.

The London Conference was held between 3 and 7 September 1962. Its importance lay in the fact that it debated the nature of Pugwash itself, reviewed past activities and was instrumental in setting the future structure of meetings. Invitations were sent out to the 179 living 'Pugwashites', and 72 were of them able to attend. Interestingly, these conferences received support from the Royal Society under then President Harry (later Lord) Florey. The Royal Society provided sponsorship and Rotblat was proud of the fact that he was in possession of a Royal Society chequebook.

The large attendance prompted the question of publicity, with some members of the Continuing Committee believing that all sessions should be open. Others believed that the presence of the press would inhibit free discussion. A compromise was reached: the press was invited to press conferences during and at the end of the proceedings. The conference started with a formal opening ceremony during which the physicist Nevill Mott took the chair in the presence of six signatories of the Russell–Einstein Manifesto, who were on the platform. Bertrand Russell welcomed the participants as chairman of the Continuing Committee. This was the last time he was to attend a Pugwash Conference. On that occasion Russell declared: '[O]ur common purpose is the survival of Man, which is in jeopardy. It is impossible to imagine a more important purpose.'

The Xth Conference drew a number of conclusions, the most significant of which was that it made the achievement of disarmament and permanent peace the main objective of Pugwash activity.

In 1963 Pugwash convened in Yugoslavia. This meeting, the XIth Pugwash Conference, was significant above all for its timing: only shortly before, a Partial Test Ban Treaty had been signed in Moscow. The treaty was considered to be of major importance; it marked a clear step forward in the fight for disarmament. As for the conference itself, three out of its five working groups were concerned with disarmament too. Discussions included the problems of abolition of delivery systems; of inspection and control in the first stage of disarmament; and of surprise attack. Also included were the topics of the importance of non-proliferation of nuclear weapons; the need to control the transfer of fissile material; and the need for a Test Ban Treaty.

The XIIth Conference was mainly of strategic importance, because it was held in India where the Ist Conference had failed to occur. The conference was attended by Mrs Indira Gandhi, as Nehru was ill. It developed mainly through four large working groups, who worked along the following themes:

1 organization for collective security;
2 the implications of a wider dispersal of military power for disarmament and world security;
3 the relation between world security and the economic problems of the developing nations;
4 the priority of science and technology in the developing nations.

On this occasion China was absent. The fact was of major concern and the conference unanimously adopted the following resolution: 'The Twelfth Pugwash Conference at Udaipur greatly regrets the absence from its deliberations of any participants from the People's Republic of China and urges the Academia Sinica to send several Chinese scientists to participate in the Thirteenth and all subsequent Pugwash Conferences'. The main achievement of this conference was to stress the close relationship between world security and development and to confirm that the subject of developing nations came within the purview of Pugwash.

The XIIIth Conference, held in 1964, featured a special working group on biological weapons. This meeting was the first in a series subsequently organized by the Study Group on Biological Warfare. During the conference, the Swedish participants announced the decision of their government to set up an international institute for research on peace-related problems.

The XIVth Conference received and accepted a detailed report from the Study Group on Biological Warfare. The report concluded that a total ban on biological as well as on nuclear weapons must be accomplished if the final aim – complete and general disarmament – is to be achieved under vigilant international verification. This group was of the view that, with further research, the destructive potential of biological weapons could eventually equal that of nuclear weapons. It also brought home the fact that, once developed, biological weapons would be far cheaper and easier to produce than nuclear weapons; thus this destructive power would be available to many countries. The conference acknowledged the suffering of the Vietnamese people, and all participants agreed that means should be sought to achieve the earliest restoration of peace in this area; the United Nations should do everything in their power to bring this about. Prompted by the events in Vietnam, the conference also considered the use of gas in war and concluded that there is much wisdom in the public reaction to the most limited use of gas, even when the effects of such use are believed to be only short-term incapacitation. One conclusion was that what is incapacitating to a healthy adult can be fatal for the young or infirm. The point was also made that, if such weapons became generally available, they would be used against civilian populations, where more destructive weapons were not allowed; and thus civilians would come to be subjected to military action, which should never be the case. This meeting can be seen as part of the growing political involvement of Pugwash and in some circles it increased controversy about Pugwash activities.

The XVth Conference, held in Addis Ababa in 1965, addressed the problem of the huge disparities in wealth between developed and developing countries. This was a significant change which signaled a shift in focus, away from disarmament and the East–West conflict. The four working groups developed the following themes:

1   education in developing countries;
2   organization of scientific institutions and research in developing countries;
3   scientific approach to aiding developing countries;
4   special problems in developing countries – including international aspects of development, development planning, industrialization, food and people, protein and nutrition, water development and conservation.

The key recommendations were for a massive programme for the training of science teachers in developing countries, the importance of the integration of science and scientists into government, the encouragement of scientists from developed countries to work in developing countries and the development and conservation of natural resources.

The XVI Conference, held in 1966, returned to the key topic of disarmament, especially in Europe. The working-group topics were as follows:

1   disarmament in Europe;
2   reduction of tensions and political settlements in Europe;
3   main problems of progress towards general and complete disarmament;
4   measures for arms limitation.

Other issues discussed included the proposal of a freeze on nuclear weapons; non-proliferation; denuclearization; military forces and conventional weapons in Europe; and observation posts.

In 1968 Pugwash took up office space in a flat in Great Russell Square, London. There was a plan at the time to extend the British Library and the building which housed this flat was purchased by the government for that purpose; but when plans changed and the site of the new library turned out to be St Pancras, the building in question was sold to the Borough of Camden. Pugwash was offered basement accommodation in the same building. It moved temporarily to the adjacent building and it is still there.

Rotblat helped to coordinate local anti-bomb groups in north London. The activity of these groups was a catalyst in the formation of the Campaign for Nuclear Disarmament (CND) in early 1958, when Canon John Collins took the organizational lead.

Bertrand Russell was appointed president of the CND. He believed that the campaign and Pugwash should exist as separate entities and should divide jobs between them, the former taking a public position and the latter operating essentially in private. Although chairman of Pugwash, Russell was not active in it. On the other hand, at least according to Rotblat, he himself was not technically a member of the CND; he had not spoken at any of its meetings, he avoided involvement and he kept his distance. He believed that the CND was a communist-front organization and he clearly wished to separate himself from it. But Russell wanted public action, and the 'Committee of 100' was formed to facilitate it. Very public marches to the nuclear weapons establishment at Aldermaston were undertaken, with Russell taking part, and Rotblat too on some occasions. Rotblat would visit Russell after Pugwash meetings, to keep him informed; but Russell did question his position as chairman. In 1962 there was a Pugwash Conference in London, as we have seen, and on that occasion Rotblat decided to invite the surviving signatories of the Russell–Einstein Manifesto. The London Conference was, with some regret, Russell's last formal involvement in Pugwash.

Cyrus Eaton continued to be involved in Pugwash, but there were tensions. Eaton wanted Pugwash activities to be more public and encouraged press participation. He moved away from his initial position of acting essentially as a host and financier without being personally involved. The 1959 Pugwash meeting discussed chemical and biological warfare, and the conclusion was that nuclear weapons presented the greater threat. Yet Eaton was of the opposite view, that chemical and biological weapons carried the greater threat; thus he became, in Rotblat's view, an interventionist. Eaton became increasingly active politically; along with this development, he came to desire US/Soviet collaboration. He was on friendly terms with President Khrushchev – the two of them exchanged gifts. He was awarded the Lenin Prize and was voted American Businessman of the Year. Yet he appeared to be speaking for Pugwash. The Continuing Committee was so concerned about his involvement with the Soviets that they wished to drop the name 'Pugwash', but Rotblat opposed this proposal: the meeting in London in 1962 retained the reference to Pugwash in its official name, which was 'the Pugwash Conferences on Science and World Affairs'. Rotblat suggests that Eaton was becoming *persona non grata*. He died in 1995; but Pugwash maintained good relationships with his widow, and the twenty-fifth anniversary meeting was held in Pugwash.

The conference had difficulties with western governments, some of which perceived it to be a communist-front organization. It was investigated by a Senate Committee, and one view which was put across on that occasion was that perhaps the conference was somewhat naïve. There was a widespread belief that individual Soviets attending the meetings were other than scientists and that they infiltrated them politically in this way. The Soviets themselves organized a meeting to discuss disarmament and Pugwash was invited; but Rotblat was against attending that meeting on the grounds that it was a politically motivated action and did not even send an observer.

After the Moscow meeting, western governments started to become aware that Pugwash was not a communist front and that its attendees were not communist jupes. There followed attempts on the part of the government to influence Pugwash and to impose the names of certain invitees, but Rotblat resisted all such attempted interventions. He tried, nevertheless, to work with the government and was awarded the CBE ('Commander of the Order of the British Empire') in 1965. He noticed, however, that the letter which accompanied this offer was signed by Harold McMillan and not by Harold Wilson. Pugwash funding was a significant issue, and Rotblat secured support from foundations such as the Carnegie Foundation and the Joseph Rowntree Foundation.

Rotblat relates how, around this time, the publisher Robert Maxwell tried to establish a *Journal of Arms Control*. Rotblat was suspicious of Maxwell and distanced himself from the *Journal*, which subsequently failed.

Rotblat described Pugwash as an amorphous organization; crucially the participants were acting as individuals and not as representatives of any institution. This was in fact a consequence of the most basic founding principle of Pugwash: participants attended as individuals and not as representatives of any government. Observers from organizations such as the United Nations or UNESCO were, however, welcome. Pugwash has never cultivated extensive publicity, but it has been highly influential. It has intervened for instance in the Cuban missile crisis in October 1962. During that crisis, the US Pugwash Group asked Rotblat to send a message to the Soviet Pugwash Group requesting them to contact the Soviet government and to persuade it that ships heading towards Cuba should be diverted elsewhere. Rotblat was in constant communication with the Soviet and the US governments, as he intended to arrange a meeting of scientists; but that meeting was no longer needed because the crisis abated. Apart from this, Pugwash can claim to have been instrumental in achieving the agreement in 1963 on the Partial Test Ban Treaty. Pugwash can also be credited with helping to establish links between the US and Vietnam in the late 1960s; the negotiation of the 1972 Biological Weapons Convention; and the Anti-Ballistic Missile Treaty in 1972. More specifically, credit for these landmark achievements should go to Rotblat.

Rotblat took the lead in guiding Pugwash through the difficulties of the Cold War, and this can be attributed to the structure of his organization. He always approached problems like a scientist, on the basis of research and systematic study. He, together with Bertrand Russell, adhered to the view that participants must attend the Pugwash Conferences as individuals, bringing in their expert knowledge and a wide range of political views. He resisted attempts on the part of governments to influence the discussions and the outcomes of the conferences. He refers to occasions where Soviet translators attempted to change the phrasing of comments and sentences, until they were caught out. Rotblat reminisces, in 2001, of a time in 1960 when the leader of the Soviet Pugwash Group, Alexander Topchiev, presented to the Continuing Committee a request to the effect that Pugwash should send delegates to a proposed world congress on disarmament. Rotblat vigorously opposed this request, as it compromised the independence of Pugwash. He wrote that '[Topchiev] was a member of the Communist Party, but he realised the importance [of Pugwash] as a channel of communication between East and West and the overriding need for it not to lose credibility in the West'. He emphasized that independence was not easy to maintain, but the conference has managed it throughout the years.

The structure of Pugwash was a great part of its strength. Pugwash was influential in the 1972 Anti-Ballistic Missile (ABM) Treaty, where the challenge was to convince the Soviets that, in a nuclear world, defensive weapons are destabilizing. At the 1964 Pugwash Conference in India, the physicist Mikhail Millionshchikov argued that the Soviet Union should have defenses. This claim was counter-argued at the same conference and became a key topic of debate at the subsequent one. Finally, Millionshchikov argued against these defensive systems at the 1969 Conference. The ABM talks in Helsinki started shortly afterwards. As an outcome of these talks, the ABM Treaty was very much influenced by Pugwash. Later on Millionshchikov confessed that he had come round to the ABM position, privately, even at the 1964 meeting, where he had argued against it. However, there may be something to the view that this represents an oversimplification. The process leading to the ABM Treaty was a complicated affair which started in the early 1960s. It has been pointed out that another group, the Soviet–American Disarmament Study Group, also played a significant part in this process. This was a bilateral working group under the leadership of two Pugwashites – Paul Doty of Harvard University and Millionshchikov himself.

The 1964 meeting discussed the ban on nuclear testing, and the Soviets appeared to be sensitive at least to the proposed inspection of nuclear sites. Pugwash was instrumental in finding a solution which involved the independent monitoring of seismic activity to indicate the testing of a bomb. A proposal to this effect was worked out at the Pugwash Conference of 1962 by three Soviet scientists and three US scientists: it involved using sealed 'black boxes' which could measure remote seismic activity. On this occasion Rotblat noted that 'the small size of the meeting, the standing of the participants, and the fact that the meeting was completely private, made it possible to conduct a detailed, erudite and fruitful discussion on the whole subject' (BLSA). The group produced a document the contents of which were made available to the governments concerned. The view, shared by Rotblat with many others, was that this document helped substantially towards reaching an agreement on a partial test-ban treaty some three months later. It has been pointed that the 'black box' proposal was discussed in correspondence between Kennedy and Khrushchev; and, if the political will to achieve it was a reality in 1964, then adopting this solution could be a crucial part of the verification process.

In the mid-1980s Pugwash debated non-offensive defence. The central idea was to find out how conventional forces could be remodelled so as to seem less threatening to one's enemy. The debate concentrated on whether it was reasonable to call for the removal of US nuclear weapons from western Europe until the huge concentration of Soviet conventional forces in eastern Europe was restructured or the troops were removed. Pugwash set up a Study Group on Conventional Forces and eventually raised the issue with President Gorbachev in 1987. Gorbachev withdrew 10,000 Soviet tanks from eastern Europe, and this in turn was of assistance in bringing about the Conventional Forces in Europe Treaty. Gorbachev has in fact written about his involvement with Rotblat. He says that he had heard of him, and of Pugwash, when things were not going well for those concerned with nuclear disarmament. Here are some of his remarks:

> [I]t is to their great credit that even then, they never succumbed to panic or despair and continued to work persistently to make people and politicians understand the pernicious futility of the confrontation and the need to rethink international politics in the nuclear age. Among those pioneering of the new thinking, Professor Rotblat always stood out for the courage of his convictions and the strength of his arguments. (Braun et al. (eds), 2007, p. 145)

Gorbachev goes on to say that in the 1980s, as change came to the Soviet Union, this 'rethinking' was given a chance to be put to the test. He himself took the initiative of putting on the political agenda the idea of achieving a world free from nuclear weapons, and he gave credit to the work done in previous years by Rotblat and Pugwash. Gorbachev also stressed the importance of the anti-war and anti-nuclear movements — especially during the Cold War, which came to an end thanks to the joint efforts of the East and West. He pointed out that the key moment was a US–Soviet summit in Geneva where the leaders of the two nations declared that a 'nuclear war cannot be won and must never be fought'. This statement functions as a test of sorts for governments which possess nuclear weapons; for it becomes then possible to see whether it represented a true, really held belief or just vacuous talk.

Change began to appear. The first was the Treaty on Intermediate-Range Forces, which eliminated two categories of nuclear weapons. The second was a treaty on strategic nuclear weapons which cut their numbers by half. However, Gorbatchev points out that we have witnessed a failure in political leadership, as the opportunities for peace offered by the end of the Cold War have not been realized. He remarks that

> the ABM Treaty has been abrogated; the requirements for effective verification and irreversibility of nuclear arms reductions have been weakened; the treaty on comprehensive cessation of nuclear weapons tests has not been ratified by all nuclear powers. And, most importantly, the goal of the eventual elimination of nuclear weapons has been essentially forgotten. What is more, the military doctrines of major powers have re-emphasized nuclear weapons as an acceptable means of war fighting, to be used in a first or even in a pre-emptive strike. (Braun et al. (eds), 2007, p. 146)]

Then he goes on to say that The Nuclear Non-Proliferation Treaty is under considerable strain. The emergence of India and Pakistan as nuclear-weapon states, the North Korean nuclear programme and the concerns surrounding the possible emergence of Iran as a nuclear power are evidence for this. There is also the terrifying prospect of nuclear weapons falling under the control of terrorists, which can only be prevented by the total abolition of nuclear weapons.

Originally the Continuing Committee of Pugwash consisted of five people: three from the UK, one from the US and one from all the Soviet-block countries. The Soviets were content with this arrangement as long as the UK was taking the lead and not the US (that would have been unacceptable). Pugwash was essentially born in the UK, so this arrangement worked well. The Continuing Committee grew in numbers until it became a council, which meets once a year. There is also an Executive Committee, which is responsible for selecting the people invited to attend meetings. The secretary general, who has a major influence on this process, is essentially the executive officer and most activities rely upon him. Rotblat was secretary general from 1957 to 1973. The president is largely a figurehead; the first one had been Sir John Cockcroft, who died shortly after being appointed, as did the second, Lord Florey. The condition, or rather stipulation, was that the president should be a Nobel Laureate; but this condition could not be maintained when

Rotblat was appointed president in 1988. Under Rotblat's presidency of the Pugwash Group, national groups were set up. Fees were paid to the international group: the UK paid $10,000 and the US and the Soviets paid $25,000 each. But after the end of the Cold War and the break-up of the Soviet Union the scientific community was demoralized and had difficulty in meeting this financial commitment.

9 | World Government

At the Pugwash Conference in Berlin in 1992, Rotblat delivered an important talk on world government (see Appendix 5). I shall discuss this paper in some detail, as it gives useful insights into his political views and general stance.

Both Einstein and Russell were advocates of world government. The manifesto did not explicitly discuss this concept, but it pointed out that 'the abolition of war will demand distasteful limitations of national sovereignty'. The manifesto stopped short of calling for a world government. However, the world itself changed with the disintegration of the Soviet Union. The US regarded nuclear weapons, from their very inception, as a means of waging ideological warfare. The bomb was developed for the purpose of subduing the Soviets. As an inevitable result, the Soviets themselves developed the bomb, and the arms race started.

Niels Bohr (whose close friendship with Rotblat at Los Alamos has been touched upon in a previous chapter) predicted the consequences of an arms race as early as 1944. He believed in openness – not only in science, but also in politics and national security. He was reported to say: '[I]t must be realized that full mutual openness only can effectively promote confidence and guarantee common security.' But Bohr's advice was not heeded. Bohr even suggested that the Soviet Union should be informed about the bomb before it was used by the US and that they should work together to exploit the potential of nuclear energy. Franklin Roosevelt was sympathetic to this plan, but Churchill rejected it out of hand. After Hiroshima and Nagasaki other scientists sought ways to prevent such catastrophic consequences, but it is true to say that Pugwash proved the most influential. In 1945, the physicist James Franck headed a group of Chicago scientists who urged the US government not to use the bomb against Japan but to demonstrate its destructive power on an uninhabited island. The suggestion was rejected; but the Frank Report did argue that the most compelling argument for an efficient organisation for peace is the existence of nuclear weapons (Braun et al. (eds), 2007, p. 291; discussed in Frisch 1979, pp. 96–7 and Badash 1995, p. 83). The Frank Report inspired other reports, which urged the disclosure of information as a firm basis for security. In the long term, there can be no international control and no international cooperation that does not presuppose an international community of knowledge.

Rotblat was very approving of Michael Gorbachev: the latter advocated new ways of thinking which had been pioneered by Pugwash. For instance, Gorbachev wrote:

> [T[he new political outlook calls for the recognition of one more simple axiom: security is indivisible. It is either equal security for all or none at all . . . The security of each nation should be coupled with the security of all members of the world community . . . Consequently, there should be no striving for security for oneself at the expense of others. (Braun et al. (eds), 2007, pp. 145–7)

Gorbachev introduced the principle of 'transparency', *glasnost*. As Rotblat points out, the removal of an oppressive Soviet regime gave impetus to states seeking independence. But this could well give rise also to new conflict and military confrontation. Rotblat's view was that 'there can be no lasting solution to it as long as the present concept of the nation–state persists, and the problem has become acute after the recent changes in the political configuration' (ibid., p. 145).

A basic principle of the United Nations is the sovereignty of its member nations. Rotblat, Pugwash and many others support any efforts to bring about freedom and justice. However, newly emerging nations rarely have democratically elected governments. Even if a recently established nation–state adopts in principle democracy as a form of government, it is rare that its government will in fact be viable. Rotblat was firmly of the view that the continuous division into many separate units flies in the face of the advances of science and technology, which have rendered the concept of the independent, sovereign nation–state obsolete. Just as in the past technological progress compelled the transition from fiefdom to the nation–state, so now the further technological advances dictate the replacement of the nation–state by a global entity. (Appendix 5)]

In the past, it was possible for small communities to lead an independent existence, since self-sustainment required little communication and cooperation with other communities. Such independence is now difficult to imagine. Modern transport and communications make isolation almost impossible. Rotblat argues that 'thanks to the progress of science the world has become significantly interdependent: anything happening in one part of the globe may have an effect in any other part'.

Ironically, the same science that improves our lives provides the means to destroy mankind. Precisely because science has given a new meaning to interdependence, 'if we do not learn to live together, we shall perish together'. Rotblat interprets this state of things as follows: '[F]rom science we have received a warning to behave ourselves. And to science we should turn to provide the guidelines for proper behaviour. The main characteristics of science are universality and openness, and I believe that their adoption in the political arena will help to reduce incentives to war' (Appendix 5).

In his talk, Rotblat also outlined some differences between science and politics. Science appears to have immutable laws and universal validity; there is no corresponding principle governing relations between nations – or at least none was detectable so far. But Rotblat suggests that such a principle may now exist: it is the survival of mankind. This idea emerges from science. Survival of the species is a fundamental driving force in the world. In the case of humans, their degree of scientific or artistic – say, musical – development extends this law of survival to aspects of civilization too . Our potential to destroy ourselves as a species is a newly discovered feature, and 'this new threat provides the motivation for the world community to organize itself in a way that would prevent such a catastrophe, as well as serving as the basis for a universal organizational structure'. Assuming that we have a common interest in maintaining civilization, this calls for a global approach to security issues. There is a requirement for the members of all nations to acknowledge a duty to the world community, to accept a loyalty to mankind and to recognize the need to be citizens of the world.

Rotblat continued:

> [A]t present, loyalty to one's nation is supreme: it overrides the loyalty to any subgroup, such as the family, local community or enforced by national laws. These laws impose limitations on our freedom, but this is the price paid for the protection provided by the state against outside enemies. Hitherto, the human species was not thought to need protection, because threats from natural causes, such as a collision with a large meteorite, were seen to have a low probability. But now the threat comes from inside, from the action of man: an abrupt end in a nuclear war, or slow extinction by poisoning the environment. Laws to protect us all are therefore urgently called for. (Appendix 5)

Hence Rotblat calls for the creation, within an international framework, of a federal government endowed with legislative powers and security forces. Such a body would probably be an extension of the United Nations. As early as 1946, Einstein had expressed the view that the United Nations was important mainly as a transitional organization, on the way towards establishing a body with sufficient legislative and executive powers to preserve the peace. Russell too upheld the view that it was technically possible to establish a world government able to exert influence – and even power, if need be. He believed that armed resistance would be fruitless. However, when he wrote on this topic in 1963, he also observed that the polarization among (and opposition between) communist and non-communist nations made such an outcome difficult to represent in practice. But that obstacle had now been removed. The United Nations was playing an important part in world security. Now Rotblat made it clear that additional legislative powers and security forces would be needed.

There is an air of *naïveté* about Rotblat's call for a world government. First, sovereign nations are very reluctant to give up their independence; in my view, many of them simply would not do it. Second, what would be the device to stop such a government from falling into other than benign hands? If a worldwide dictatorship were to occur, it would not have the checks and balances inherent in the present organization of political structures, where nation states attempt to cooperate and intervene to defend or protect. Third, there would be a vast, in fact probably unaccountable, bureaucracy. Rotblat's attitude sprang from his concentration on the dangers inherent in the present division and organization of the world; and this way of thinking led him to believe that we have no alternative but to change that division and organization completely.

At a Pugwash Conference in Norway, an American was appointed secretary general just after Rotblat stepped down from the position of president in 1997. This was in breach of the unwritten rule that the post of secretary general should not be occupied by any member from the US or from the Soviet Union. By this time Rotblat was growing more and more frustrated with the Pugwash organization, but said that he 'should not interfere too much' with his 'baby' (BLSA).

The problem was that there was now a fundamental disagreement between Pugwash and him. He believed it was right that, during the Cold War, the emphasis was upon limiting the proliferation of nuclear weapons and arms control through the use of treaties. After the end of the Cold War the aim of Pugwash, according to Rotblat, should be total disarmament, the abolition of all nuclear weapons and of all war. This view was supported, but not by all the members of Pugwash.

10 | Fallout from Pugwash and Post-Retirement Activities

Rotblat described his career as follows: twenty years in nuclear physics, thirty years in medical physics and forty years in Pugwash. He referred to his activities after his retirement as a professor at St Bart's as 'the fallout' from Pugwash. During this period he devoted the best part of his time to Pugwash, but also became involved in other important activities. The Swedish government desired to celebrate the fact that Sweden had not been at war for one hundred and fifty years, and approached him for ideas in this direction. Rotblat thought that a peace institute would be just the thing. But this was not to be an institute built on the model of already existing institutions; it had to be a novel one, based on science and dedicated to finding out exactly how many nuclear weapons were held by each nation. This institute became known as the Stockholm International Peace Research Institute (the SIPRI). It continues to be financed by the government and produces a yearbook which is the most authoritative source of information on this subject. The first director of SIPRI was a Cambridge economist. He was followed by Frank Barnaby, the first paid Pugwash employee – in Pugwash his position was of executive secretary. Rotblat was very critical of his appointment at SIPRI: he thought that Barnaby was not up to the job because he had poor organizational skills.

As a consequence of his involvement in SIPRI, Rotblat was approached by the World Health Organization (WHO) for the assessment of the effects of radiation in warfare. In 1984 he produced a report which was accepted by the WHO. This report pointed out that, in addition to the blast and radiation effects associated with the use of nuclear weapons, there was an electromagnetic pulse which would interrupt vast amounts of communications. The notion of a 'nuclear winter' was formulated there and the facts described for the first time. The sun's rays would be effectively blocked by the amount of ground material propelled into the atmosphere by the explosion of the nuclear weapon, and this would result in a cooling of the earth. In 1987 Rotblat was involved in producing a second report, which focused on the effects of radiation following the use of nuclear weapons. A study of people exposed to radiation on account of unusually high levels of thorium – a radioactive gas which occurs in nature – had been conducted in Kerela, India. However, no significant conclusions were reached. The population studied was migrant and the relevant data was difficult to collect. The largest population exposed to radiation was that of the survivors of Hiroshima and Nagasaki. So Rotblat traveled to Japan. He had predicted an increase incidence of leukaemias among these survivors; but his experiments on mice also indicated that exposure to radiation resulted in the initiation of many different types of disease, and that these cancers and the associated genetic disorders may take up to twenty or thirty years to appear.

Knowing these facts from his earlier work, Rotblat argued for the continuous reduction of acceptable dosage levels for all those who worked with radiation: there was no 'safe' level of exposure. This was to prove a crucial finding which, when it percolated down, changed attitudes to many screening programmes in general use in the NHS at the time. From then on, medical authorities accepted that routine procedures such as chest X-rays should no longer be performed. There should be very specific and strict indications for each X-ray. Anyone around fifty in the UK would probably be horrified to reflect on the number of children who used to be exposed to unnecessary X-rays when trying on their new school shoes.

As we have seen, when the Cold War ended Rotblat wanted Pugwash to return to campaigning for a world free of nuclear weapons. He was approached by the Australian foreign minister, who declared that his government desired just such a world. The Canberra Commission was set up which comprised seventeen people and worked for two years. A significant contribution came from General Lee Butler, who had commanded US nuclear forces but after retirement took up an anti-nuclear stance. However, the support for this commission and for the position it promoted declined after the election and change of government in Australia.

Rotblat remarks that during this period he started to be accepted by what he terms the establishment. Other awards followed his CBE in 1965. He won the Einstein Peace Prize in 1992 and donated to Pugwash the $20,000 which came with it. Finally, he was elected as a Fellow of The Royal Society (FRS) in 1995. This election was in the offing when he was still working as a nuclear physicist at Liverpool, but the proposal was withdrawn when he decided to move into the field of medical physics (Chadwick told him straight out that this decision would cost him his FRS). When he eventually received his Royal Society Fellowship, he remarked that 'it had taken a long time to forgive' his 'sins' – that is, the sin of leaving nuclear physics – and that the honour of this election had been 'denied' him 'for so many years'.

The award of the Nobel Prize for Peace in 1995 was of huge personal significance to Rotblat. The Peace Prize is unique in that it can be awarded to organizations as well as to individuals; for example the Red Cross has been a recipient. Rotblat received it jointly with the Pugwash Conferences. The circumstances surrounding this award are somewhat amusing. He knew that he had been nominated by the International Peace Bureau, but in 1995 there was a general agreement that it would be awarded to John Major for his peace efforts in Northern Island. This was the subject of much press speculation at the time. The announcement was to be made at noon, Stockholm time, on Friday 13 October – which in UK was 11 a.m., on the last day of the Conservative Party Conference. A space had been reserved around this time within the morning proceedings for a speech designed to acknowledge the award. Rotblat was in the Pugwash office in London when a telephone call was received earlier that morning saying that he, along with Pugwash, had been awarded the Nobel Prize for Peace. He was stunned; the award came to him as a complete surprise. Later he found out that John Major was not even on the shortlist (BLSA). He remembers going out for a walk to collect his thoughts and being confronted by a radio-car for an interview on his return to the office. Crowds had gathered, too – on the rumour that Princess Diana was being interviewed! A press conference was organized at the neighbouring Imperial Hotel and afterwards Rotblat gave interviews to the BBC and to ITV News, losing his voice in the process.

The circumstances surrounding the award of the Nobel Prize for

Peace are worth recounting: they held a particular place in Rotblat's affection. He received the prize in Oslo and not Stockholm because, at the time of the inception of the ceremony, Norway was part of Sweden and this location of the proceedings was a form of recognition. The prize was awarded by the chairman of the Nobel Committee, in the presence of the King and Queen of Norway. One of the requirements is that the successful candidates should give a talk on the day of receiving the prize. On this occasion Rotblat delivered a very powerful speech, entitled 'Remember your humanity' (Appendix 6). He received a standing ovation, including from the royal couple. The speech reiterated the dangers of nuclear weapons and launched an appeal to scientists to take responsibility for their work and to end all forms of war. Rotblat began by stating that he was speaking as a scientist and human being. He stressed that the decision to use nuclear weapons against Japan at the close of the Second World War and the subsequent build-up of nuclear arsenals was made by governments on the basis of political and military perceptions. However, scientists on both sides of the of the iron curtain played a significant role in maintaining the momentum of the nuclear arms race throughout the four decades of the Cold War. Rotblat quotes a most perceptive comment by Lord Zuckerman, for many years chief scientific adviser to the British government:

> when it comes to nuclear weapons . . . it is the man in the laboratory who [is] at the start of the process that for this or that arcane reason it would be useful to improve an old or to devise a new nuclear warhead. It is he, the technician, not the commander in the field, who is at the heart of the arms race. (Braun et al. (eds), 2007, p. 217)

Rotblat was at pains to point out that the very first resolution of the United Nations, adopted unanimously, called for the elimination of nuclear weapons. Moreover, there was a legal requirement from the five official nuclear nations to act on this resolution – a requirement made when they signed the Non-Proliferation Treaty. The nuclear powers have committed themselves to complete nuclear disarmament.

However, Rotblat points out that these declared aims are not matched by the policies and actions of the states in question. Since the end of the Cold War, the Soviets and the US started to reduce the number of nuclear weapons in their respective arsenals, but Rotblat was very pessimistic about the prospects of reducing nuclear arsenals to zero. The principle of deterrence was still in place, and he saw it as a continuation of the Cold War. We are somehow led to believe that there is something good about the existence of nuclear weapons, insofar as they prevented another world war; and not only that, but all kinds of war. This very idea was anathema to Rotblat: to him, the main point about the existence and availability of nuclear weapons was quite different. He himself confessed that the Cuban missile crisis terrified him. Millions could have been killed, and it rested entirely with Nikita Khrushchev to abide or not by a US ultimatum. Rotblat warned: '[T]his is the reality of nuclear weapons: they may trigger a world war; a war which, unlike previous ones, destroys all of civilization.'

As for the argument that nuclear weapons prevent non-nuclear wars, Rotblat was totally dismissive of that too. He pointed out that, since 1945, tens of millions have died in many wars, and that nuclear states were involved in a number of them. There is no evidence that a world without nuclear weapons would be a more dangerous world. We must simply get rid of all nuclear weapons. Rotblat acknowledged that this goal would take time, but there were steps we could take. Nuclear weapons exist to deter nuclear attack. All nuclear weapons states should recognize, in a treaty, that they will never be the first to use them. This would then allow for a gradual reduction in nuclear arsenals.

Rotblat also appealed to scientists. Some scientists, he said, try to avert the dangers resulting from science and technology, but many of them see science as being in some sense 'neutral'. Rotblat asked, 'should any scientist work on weapons of mass destruction?' and quoted Hans Bethe, director of the Theory Division at Los Alamos, saying a clear 'no'. On the occasion of the fiftieth anniversary of Hiroshima, Bethe declared:

[A]s the director of the Theoretical Division at Los Alamos, I participated at the most senior level in the World War II Manhattan Project that produced the first atomic weapons.

Now, at age 88, I am one of the few remaining such senior persons alive. Looking back at the half century since that time, I feel the most intense relief that these weapons have not been used since World War II, mixed with the horror that tens of thousands of such weapons have been built since that time – one hundred times more than any of us at Los Alamos could ever have imagined.

Accordingly, I call on all scientists in all countries to cease and

desist from work creating, developing, improving and manufacturing further nuclear weapons – and, for that matter, other
weapons of potential mass destruction such as chemical and biological weapons. (Appendix 6)

Rotblat also highlighted the fact that vigilance is required in other areas
of research, for example in some industrial and government research,
which sometimes presents misleading information to the public. He
agued that 'whistle-blowing' should be part of the scientific ethos. His
talk ended with the following statement:

the quest for a war-free world has a basic purpose: survival. But if in
the process we learn how to achieve it by love rather than by fear,
by kindness rather than by compulsion; if in the process we learn to
combine the essential with the enjoyable, the expedient with the
benevolent, the practical with the beautiful, this will be an extra
incentive to embark on this great task. Above all, remember your
humanity.

However, this award was not without controversy: some of those
opposed to nuclear disarmament protested. Within the UK press there
were hostile people; the Sunday Telegraph suggested that perhaps
Rotblat should be imprisoned. He received half of the financial reward,
$500,000, while the same amount went to Pugwash. But Rotblat
signed most of his financial settlement over to Pugwash: one third to
International Pugwash, one third to the British Pugwash Group and
one third to a Foundation created to fund special Pugwash projects. He
was subsequently knighted, receiving the KCMG ('Knight
Commander of the Order of St Michael and St George') – of which he
said, mischievously, that within the civil service it was known as
'kindly call me god'. Once again he was subject to press criticism; in
particular, the *Daily Telegraph* asked why a former member of the CND
was awarded this honour. Then Rotblat was made an Honorary Fellow
of The Academy of Medical Sciences and took great pride in this nom-
ination, as he was not trained in medicine. He was also made an
Honorary Fellow of The Institute of Physics.

These many awards did not dampen his enthusiasm for influencing
the young. He was eager to speak in schools and addressed the sixth-

formers at Eton and Harrow. He claimed that sixth-formers asked the most perceptive and interesting questions. He felt that towards the end of his life he was finally accepted, especially in Poland, where he was fêted after the award of the Nobel Prize. Indeed his portrait hangs next to that of Madame Curie in the Polish Embassy in London. He received the Polish Order of Merit with Star, was made a foreign member of the Polish Academy of Science and was awarded the Copernicus Medal.

Rotblat remained politically active to the end of his life, and I will discuss at some length his views on the Iraq War and on the Bush Administration. Before embarking on that I will explore, by way of introduction, his efforts to argue the case for Mordechai Vanunu in Tel Aviv in October 1996. These are highly illustrative of his humanitarian approach to life, which permeated almost everything he did.

Mordechai Vanunu was a whistle-blower who disclosed to the whole world Israel's nuclear activities at the Dimona nuclear reprocessing plant. He was sentenced to eighteen years in solitary confinement. Rotblat began his talk on Vanunu at the Conference on Democracy, Human Rights and Mordechai Vanunu (Tel Aviv, 14–15 October 1996; reprinted in Braun et al. (eds), 2007, 'The crime and punishment of Mordecai Vanunu', p. 232) by saying:

> [W]e are here for the sake of one man. Mordechai Vanunu. Forty-two years old yesterday, he has been lingering in Ashkelon prison for a quarter of his life, in solitary confinement. Our mission is to plead for the restoration of his freedom on humanitarian grounds. But in presenting our plea, we have to examine the motivation and the consequences of his deed; we have to look into the crime and punishment of Mordechai Vanunu.

Rotblat concedes from the outset that, by disclosing Israel's secret development of nuclear weapons, Vanunu had committed a punishable offence under Israeli law. As he points out, this was a classic case of a familiar dilemma, in the particular form it faces individuals in our nuclear age. In this case, the dichotomy was between the undertaking – made by Vanunu in writing – not to divulge the nature of the work he was engaged in and his belief that the outcome of his work – the production of nuclear weapons – presented a threat to mankind which required him to act otherwise.

Israel had not signed the Non-Proliferation Treaty (NPT). The government argued that Israel was in a particular situation, being a nation surrounded by hostile states. Hence Israel insisted that it had to possess nuclear weapons as an ultimate deterrent. Rotblat, on the other hand, was firmly of the view that, far from bringing security to Israel, these weapons were a new source of danger, and to the whole of the Middle East. They created a fundamental imbalance, prompting other nations to feel that they, too, must acquire nuclear weapons of their own. Rotblat claims:

> [W]e have to remember that this is not an issue of concern to just one region. It is a matter of concern to all people. It is not yet generally appreciated that a full scale nuclear war may destroy not only our civilization but the whole of the human race. Any use of nuclear weapons, anywhere, carries the risk of escalating to a much wider use, and threatening everybody on the globe.

He argues that the general public must be kept informed as to what is going on: we are all entitled to know about activities which put at risk our lives and those of future generations. The task of providing this information is incumbent primarily on scientists and technologists, largely because they are most likely to be the first to know. This was the driving force that compelled Vanunu to divulge information on the development of nuclear weapons. Rotblat puts it across that Vanunu should not be seen as a traitor to his country but as a sincere, if misguided, whistle-blower who attempted to bring to public attention the potential dangers of Israel's possession of nuclear weapons.

Somewhat contentiously, Rotblat proceeds from here to argue that whistle-blowing should be part of the ethos of scientists and should become an accepted form of social behaviour:

> [T]he convention on the abolition of nuclear weapons – which I hope will be agreed in the next few decades – should contain a clause mandating every country to pass national laws that would make it the right and duty of every citizen to notify an international authority about any attempt to violate the convention. Such legislation would provide immunity to whistle-blowers.

Rotblat also argues that the sentence did not match the crime. He returns for comparison to the Klaus Fuchs affair – 'the crime of the century, because of their immense impact on the whole course of world affairs'. As he points out, Vanunu told the story of the Dimona installation openly, to the whole world, while Fuchs relayed information in secret, to an enemy regime notorious for its suppression of the freedom of information. Vanunu brought to the attention of the general public information which was of no real value to the enemies of Israel (since the fact that Israel possessed nuclear weapons capability was common knowledge within the nuclear community and among governments), whereas Fuchs gave the Soviets the blueprint of the Nagasaki bomb, enabling them to manufacture a bomb some years ahead of themselves. As we have seen earlier, Fuchs served only nine years in prison and was rewarded with a university chair in East Germany.

Rotblat makes the point that the main purpose of Israel's possessing a nuclear arsenal is to deter attempts to destroy the nation using conventional weapons. For this to be effective, it is clearly essential that would be enemies are aware of Israel's nuclear capability. Vanunu provided this information. Israel would probably have preferred that this information be conveyed indirectly, but the security of Israel was not compromised. Rotblat could only see that the purpose of giving Vanunu such a harsh sentence was to act as a deterrent. There is also a view that he is being held, then, in solitary confinement to prevent him revealing more information that could be harmful to Israel, but Rotblat was firmly of the opinion that he could not reveal anything that was already not widely known or published.

Rotblat remained politically active and I will discuss, his thoughts on the Iraq War and attitudes to the US. These contain many insights, and summarize something of his world vision and are thus of major significance. They bring Rotblat's opinions and strongly held beliefs directly into contemporary politics. At the Pugwash Conference in 2003, at Dalhousie University, Halifax, Nova Scotia , Canada he delivered a talk 'The Nuclear Issue: Pugwash and the Bush Policies' and I will rely heavily upon this for the following discussion (Appendix 7). He starts by saying that he wished to highlight the dangers to the world which may arise from the nuclear policies of the George W. Bush Administration. He was strongly critical of the US Administration in its conduct of world affairs. In the highly charged political atmosphere, due largely to the Iraq war, anyone criticizing the American Administration could be considered to be anti-American, but he was at pains to point out that this was not so. The thrust of his argument was that the policies of the then Bush Administration could be considered to be anti-American, as in his view, they did not represent the opinions of the majority of the American people. He believed that the US would never have been in that position had Al Gore been elected.

He pointed out that the deep divide in world opinion was a consequence of the Bush slogan 'You are either with us or against us'. This was initially applied to the campaign against al-Qaeda, but went on to include all of those who disagreed with the Bush Administration. There are many, perhaps a majority in the world, who are totally opposed to terrorism but are not at all at ease with the actions of the Bush Administration. He found the policies of Bush hypocritical and repugnant. The US proclaims itself to be the champion of democracy in the world, while imposing its will in a totally undemocratic manner. It is supposed to uphold the rule of law, yet violates legal commitments under international treaties. Rotblat goes on to say that the US berates members of the United Nations for exercising their rights under existing rules, but will take military action against a member state without the authority of the United Nations.

Bush's main criticism of the United Nations is that it is ineffective; a useless and emasculated organization that is incapable of making decisions. However, long, protracted discussions and negotiations are a characteristic of democratic systems and processes. The Bush Administration could not tolerate this, and Rotblat pointed out that this is a feature of a totalitarian regime.

The evidence for this was the war against Iraq. The justification for that war was to remove weapons of mass destruction (and we know the outcome of that). However, Rotblat felt the real reason to invade Iraq was to increase US influence in the Middle East. There is considerable evidence to show that the main reason to bring down the Sadam Hussein regime in Iraq was to change the political situation in the Middle East to give the US greater political, economic and military influence in the region, if not control. Similar threats were also made against Syria and Iran.

Rotblat went to some lengths to explore the background that

resulted in this situation. During the Cold War, neo-conservative groups within the US advocated robust foreign policies. During the Reagan Administration, these groups exerted considerable influence over the President. With the end of the Cold War and the first Gulf War seen as a job half done, the neo-conservatives became even more active. Calls were made for a new US foreign and military policy, promoting US dominance by preventing the rise of hostile nations and pre-emptive military action against states suspected of developing weapons of mass destruction (WMD). There were also calls, made by Richard Perle, for then Israeli Prime Minister Benjamin Netanyahu to pursue policies to remove Sadam Hussein and destabilize the governments of Syria, Saudi Arabia, Lebanon and Iran. Later, under the Clinton Administration, Perle called for a regime change in Iraq.

There then followed the al-Qaeda attack of 11 September. Rotblat was highly critical of attempts to gain UN Resolutions, seeing this as a charade and a cynical attempt by the US to gain legitimacy. Rotblat was of the view that the decision had been taken some time before to invade and he believed that the timing was not dictated by any outcome from the efforts of the weapons inspector, Hans Blix but rather by the time needed to assemble the necessary military hardware.

The reason given for the invasion of Iraq was the removal of WMD. This has been shown to be completely false. Rotblat called for the resignation of Prime Minister Blair if these weapons were not found. A letter is shown below that highlights the threat from Bin Laden after the attack on 9/11:

LETTER TO THE EDITOR
From Professor Sir Joseph Rotblat, FRS
The Times, 15 September 2001
Sir,
In the agonizing analysis of Tuesday's tragic events, two points need to be stressed germane to future dangers. One is the complete disregard by the perpetrators for human life, as evidenced by the choice of targets and the timing of the attacks on New York. The second is that the terrorists are a powerful organization with huge financial, manpower, and very likely technological resources. This means that much more devastating attacks cannot be excluded. One such attack could be by the use

of a biological weapon, and there are plenty of them in the world. But far worse would be the use of a nuclear device. I would not be surprised if a group like Bin Laden's had managed to acquire such a device and had already smuggled it into a city in the USA, or, indeed, in the UK. Try to imagine devastation ten, or even a hundred, times greater than we saw on Tuesday. The mind boggles. But this is a real threat. Urgent measures need to be taken to lessen the probability of this occurring, namely by reducing the availability of the materials necessary to nuclear weapons – highly enriched uranium and plutonium. There are huge quantities of weapon-grade uranium. Russia has more than 1,000 tonnes, enough to make 20,000 atom bombs. It is quite easy to render it harmless by mixing it with natural uranium. A deal was arranged some years ago between the USA and Russia to dilute 500 tonnes of the latter's uranium but, for mainly commercial reasons, this is proceeding at an incredibly slow pace (about 30 tonnes per year). President George W. Bush should authorize an acceleration of the programme. There are also large quantities of plutonium, in the USA and Russia, from the dismantlement of nuclear warheads. A programme for the disposition of the plutonium has been prepared but, according to recent reports, the design work on a US plutonium immobilization plant has been suspended, apparently for financial reasons. The Russian programme is also ailing for lack of finance. Here again President Bush should take action.

Yours faithfully,

Joseph Rotblat

True, Rotblat did say that it would be hypocritical for those who opposed the war not to 'rejoice over the downfall of a tyrannical regime, and not to admit that this would not have come about so quickly without military intervention'; yet he added that the price paid was too high. It reinstated in world affairs the maxim that the end justifies the means.

Rotblat lamented the invasion of Iraq as it was a setback to those like him, who believed that morality and adherence to the rules of law should be guiding principles. In his view, these principles were abandoned in favour of the principle that might is right and that other nations may be compelled to accept that there is now a single super power, the US, who acts as the world's policeman. He argued that even if the Americans were less arrogant in the pursuit of these ends, a system with a built-in inequality will inevitably be found to be unstable. Resentments will arise and manifest themselves in a number of ways, including an increase in international terrorism. Rotblat's hope was that internal opposition within the US would help to counter this situation, public opinion being bound to change when the dangers of the US policies became clear. Nevertheless, the problem was that these concerns may have disastrous results, especially from the nuclear doctrines of the Bush Administration – namely the end of arms control. Rotblat accepted this risk and saw that the only viable way forward was disarmament. He said that

> the elimination of nuclear weapons has always been the goal of Pugwash, following the call in the Russell–Einstein Manifesto. We have pursued this goal for moral reasons, because ethical issues have always played a major role in Pugwash: any use of nuclear weapons has been seen as immoral. But we have also seen in our goals a basic purpose: survival. Any use of nuclear weapons would carry the danger of escalation and a threat to our continued existence. (Appendix 7)

Rotblat was quite explicit about the fact that the use of nuclear weapons was contemplated by the Bush Administration. Such policies aimed to achieve two ends: a defensive strategy which would make the US invulnerable to external attack; and an offensive strategy which might threaten unfriendly nations with military action, including the use of nuclear weapons. For the defensive strategy, missile defence had priority. The US abrogated the Anti-Ballistic Missile Treaty and put in its place a massively increased budget for a missile defence project. But Rotblat was far more concerned about the offensive system, since a nuclear capability was now included in conventional war strategy and planning. This was a significant change. Rotblat commented:

> the previous doctrine of deterrence, by which the actual use of nuclear weapons was seen as a last resort, when everything else had failed, has been thrown overboard. In the new doctrine, nuclear weapons have become a standard part of military strategy; they would be used in a conflict just like any other explosives. This repre-

sents a major shift in the whole rationale for nuclear weapons. (Appendix 7)

This prospect appalled Rotblat.

The thinking behind this change in policy was that nations hostile to the US could acquire WMDs, and the US made it quite clear that it would not allow hostile nations and terrorists to threaten the US with them. The Bush Administration was prepared to go as far as the use of pre-emptives permitted. Rotblat pointed out that the US had started to design a new nuclear warhead of low yield, which was shaped in such a way that it could penetrate concrete bunkers and destroy weapons, terrorists or leaders of hostile states. Clearly, such a weapon would have to be tested. As Rotblat observed, this would contravene the Comprehensive Test Ban Treaty, but the US never signed it: the Bush Administration had nothing but contempt for international treaties and argued for the resumption of nuclear testing. This possibility of the US resuming nuclear testing was Rotblat's great fear. Should the US do it, this would be a clear signal that other nations could do the same. The first to resume testing after the US would almost certainly be China. The development of this new bomb was of particular concern to Rotblat, as it would blur the distinction between conventional and nuclear weapons. As he put it:

> [T]he chief characteristic of a nuclear weapon is its enormous destructive power, unique in comparison with current chemical or biological weaponry, also designated as WMD. This has resulted in a taboo on the use of nuclear weapons in combat, a taboo that has held out since Nagasaki. But if at one end of the spectrum a nuclear bomb can be manufactured which does not differ quantitatively from ordinary explosives, then the qualitative difference will also disappear; the nuclear threshold will be crossed, and nuclear weapons will gradually come to be seen as a tool of war, even though the danger they present to the existence of the human race will remain. (Ibid.)

The importance of the claim that the US did not rule out the pre-emptive use of nuclear weapons was of deep concern to him. To reiterate: the adoption of this position by the US, apart from its own significance, would also give other nations the license to follow – for example in the Kashmir crisis. India's officially declared position was that it would not be the first to use nuclear weapons. On the other hand, India's nuclear policies largely followed in the footsteps of the US; so, if the US retained the pre-emptive use of nuclear weapons, then India would do the same. In this case the obvious target was Pakistan. As Rotblat pointed out, comments by George Fernandes, India's then foreign minister, are on record to the effect that India had 'a much better case to go for pre-emptive action against Pakistan than the United States has in Iraq'. One could only speculate whether Pakistan and not India would be the first to use nuclear weapons.

There was also the problem of Taiwan. The US was committed to the defence of Taiwan. Should the Taiwanese government declare independence from China, this would almost certainly result in an invasion by mainland China. The US commitment to the defence of Taiwan could well result in a pre-emptive nuclear strike. Finally, there was the ongoing problem of North Korea. It seems now highly unlikely that that country would be subject to a nuclear attack, but some little time ago, when it was one of the nations on Bush's 'axis of evil', such a prospect was not inconceivable.

Rotblat was also concerned about the intentions of Japan. The Japanese Constitution declares that the Japanese people has forever renounced using force, or threatening to use it, as a means of settling international disputes. Under the President Koizumi, with US encouragement, there was a growing tendency to seek to revise the constitution in order for Japan to become a nuclear state. Japan's base in science and technology is very strong, so there would be no technological difficulties.

Rotblat remarked that, 'altogether, the aggressive policy of the United States, under the Bush Administration, has created a precarious situation in world affairs, with a greatly increased danger of nuclear weapons being used in combat'. This was the opposite of the goals of Pugwash, which had been declared and adopted at the conference of the preceding year: 'Pugwash is strongly committed to the goal of abolishing all nuclear weapons. He felt it imperative that Pugwash constantly remind the international community of the immorality, illegality, and peril inherent in nuclear weapons, and to propose concrete steps towards their elimination' (ibid.). Furthermore, Rotblat commented that any attempt to achieve these goals by persuading the Bush Administration to change its policy through argument or appeals to morality would be completely fruitless. He believed instead in a direct appeal to the American people: he saw some hope in producing a change in public opinion, given that in a democratic society policies can be changed. He advised that 'the Pugwash effort should be towards an acceleration of that process in a campaign to influence public opinion, a campaign based on principles of morality and equity'. And he continued:

> [T]he immorality in the use of nuclear weapons is taken for granted, but this is very seldom raised when calling for nuclear disarmament. We are told that a campaign based on moral principles is a non-starter, and we are afraid of appearing naïve, and divorced from reality. I see in the use of this argument evidence that we have allowed ethical considerations to be ignored for far too long. We are accused of not being realistic, when what we are trying to do is to prevent real dangers, the dangers that would result from the current policies of the Bush Administration. (Ibid.)

The other basic principle was adherence to international law: Rotblat pointed out that world peace cannot be achieved without adherence to the international treaties. Here he reiterated the background to the NPT, in which Pugwash was involved in the early years and which 98 per cent of nations had signed. In accordance with the NPT, all the member states which did not possess nuclear weapons undertook not to acquire them. In addition, those nations who had tested nuclear weapons, and hence officially possessed them, undertook to rid the world of them. Signing the NPT was a legal commitment. Rotblat was firmly of the view that the Bush Administration policy of allowing the existence and potential use of nuclear weapons was in direct breach of the NPT.

Rotblat explained how the Bush Administration had managed to convince the American people that only that part of the NPT relating to non-nuclear nations was valid, and hence that the nations which did not comply with it – Iran being the candidate there – should be admonished; and direct military intervention would not be excluded. That part of the NPT relating to nuclear nations – the injunction that they should get rid of their nuclear arsenal – was conveniently ignored by the

Administration. Rotblat quoted two highly relevant passages from newspapers. One of them read: 'at a meeting of the IAEA today, the US will urge it to declare Tehran in breach of the Non-Proliferation Treaty. The Treaty seeks to confine nuclear weapons to Russia, Britain, France, China and America' (Appendix 7). This was clearly in contravention of the NPT. Next, the *New York Times* declared, similarly, that 'it [the NPT] was established to stop the spread of nuclear weapons beyond the original declared nuclear powers of the US, China, Russia, the UK and France'. Again, there is no mentioning here of the requirement for the nations in possession of nuclear weapons to dismantle them.

The Bush Administration was firmly of the view that all WMDs – nuclear, chemical and biological – in the possession of hostile states and of terrorists represent one of the greatest security challenges facing the United States. But according to Rotblat such weapons posed exactly the same danger even when they were possessed by friendly nations. The question is: when shall we hear that even the US had agreed to dispose of its nuclear arsenal?

[W]e are facing here a basic issue in which the ethical and legal aspect are intertwined. The use of nuclear weapons is seen by the great majority of people in the world as immoral, due to their indis-criminate nature and unprecedented destructive power. Their possession – and therefore likely use – is thus equally unacceptable, whether by 'rogue' or benevolent regimes. (Ibid.)

Rotblat points out that the elimination of nuclear weapons has been the declared aim of the United Nations and resolutions are passed year after year to that effect. These resolutions are consistently ignored. One needs to reiterate, over and over again, that the US has signed and ratified an international treaty which commits it to the elimination of its own stock of nuclear weapons, yet it is clearly pursuing policies which require the retention of such weapons. There is clearly a fundamental contradiction in US policy. If the US persists in retaining nuclear weapons, then it must withdraw from the NPT. This would probably result in a large increase in the number of nuclear states. Alternatively, the US could eliminate its nuclear arsenal.

It was only very late in his life that Rotblat argued for influencing public opinion and at last seemed to grasp its significance. This was a change in his views induced through collaboration with other organizations, and it ran was counter to the way Pugwash had previously operated. Pugwash had been accused – correctly, in Rotblat's view – of being an exclusive club. Now he retracted:

> But even if our mode of work has been justified in the past, I believe that the time has come to open up. I am not advocating that Pugwash should become a mass movement; what I am suggesting is that we should be more willing to collaborate with other organizations in the sense of spearheading a large effort to provide information to the general public. Pugwash is a movement of scientists, but the job of the scientists is not only to do original research; education is an essential element of it. And this is in essence what I propose. (Ibid.)

The task of influencing public opinion could not be undertaken by Pugwash alone. The new way of working had already been taken up by the British Pugwash Group, which was collaborating with a number of organizations, including CND and Greenpeace. This was a very significant change to the way Pugwash operated.

Rotblat continued by making the following point: 'I believe in the inherent goodness of Man. What would be the point of keeping the human species if this were not true! But then our task must be to ensure that this belief gains general acceptance'. He remarked that we still conduct world affairs on the assumption that survival depends on military strength. This attitude 'completely ignores the radical changes that have occurred as a result of the advances in science and technology, changes which make such a stand no longer necessary. If equitably distributed, our resources could be sufficient to meet the basic needs of the world population, despite its huge increase.' Rotblat sums up this important paper in the following words:

> [I]n a world armed with weapons of mass destruction, the use of which might bring the whole of civilization to an end, we cannot afford a polarized community, with its inherent threat of military confrontations. In this technological age, a global, equitable community, to which we all belong as world citizens, has become a necessity.

11 | Thoughts on a Creative Life

Joseph Rotblat was not without his critics. There are those who believe, or believed, that he was a Soviet spy. There is absolutely no evidence that I can find for this claim. He was also accused of arrogance and self-seeking behaviour. His own remark that St Bartholomew's was looking to appoint 'a great scientist' was taken as evidence of such features. In my view, they were fortunate to get him.

The second linear accelerator installed at St Bart's Medical College was certainly not a success. Rotblat himself admitted that in the latter part of his career he became less active in research. He also admitted to being something of a showman – from the opening of the first accelerator at St Bart's down to his appearances on television. However, such remarks must be placed in the whole context of his achievements in science and in his quest for peace.

He was asked once in an interview what were the worst experiences of his life. His answer carried him through the hardships endured during the First World War, and above all through the suffering caused by the loss and death of his wife. He recounted his efforts to enable her to leave Poland through Denmark, with the help of Niels Bohr; then through Belgium, which was instantly invaded; and finally through Italy, which declared war on the very day she started her journey. All these attempts failed.

Among his best experiences, being enrolled as a student at the Free University (especially after having expected failure) was a high point. The Nobel Prize had come as a complete surprise – but a very welcome one. The election to the Fellowship of the Royal Society was all the more precious to him as it had been denied him for many years. He greatly enjoyed living in England; he turned down far better paid jobs in the US, preferring to live in England where he was accepted, appreciated and finally honoured. He thought that his life here was better than it could have been in Poland – he was aware that, had he returned there after the Second World War as he intended at one time, he would have had not only to endure anti-Semitism, but even his life would probably have been at risk under a Soviet regime. There was a telling interview when he appeared on the radio programme 'Desert Island Discs' in 1998. On that occasion he recounted the circumstances of his appointment as a KCMG, which cited his services to international understanding. The first recording he played on that occasion was Chopin's *Polonaise* in A flat, interpreted by John Ogden (the very same piece which his friend and colleague Otto Frisch had played for friends during their stay in Liverpool: this recalled his Polish origins and sympathies. There followed anti-war folk-songs like 'Last Night I had the Strangest Dream' and 'Where Have All the Flowers Gone' – and, interestingly, 'The Sorcerer's Apprentice', which puts one in mind of the scientist isolated in an ivory tower and oblivious to the consequences of his work. His favourite recording was Beethoven's Ninth Symphony and its 'Ode to Joy'. On Desert Island Dics he chose to take the *Encyclopaedia Britannica*, on CD ROM, on a solar-powered laptop, as he believed that there is so much to know in the world.

The greatest tribute to Rotblat that I can think of is summed up in James Chadwick's comment to John Cockcroft:

I don't know if you have met Rotblat, a Pole who has been here nine months. He is a very able man, one of the best I have come across for some years.

Appendixes

1 'Leaving the Bomb', *Bulletin of Atomic Scientists*, August 1985. Reproduced with permission.

2 The Russell–Einstein Manifesto. This was originally a Press Release.

3 Statement from the First Pugwash Conference, Pugwash, July 7–10, 1957. Reproduced by permission of the US Pugwash Group.

4 Statement from the Third Pugwash Conference, Vienna, September 14–20, 1958. Reproduced by permission of the US Pugwash Group.

5 'Time to Rethink the Idea of World Government'. This was a paper given by Rotblat at the 42nd Pugwash Conference, Berlin, 1992. Reproduced by permission of the US Pugwash Group.

6 'Remember Your Humanity'. This is his Nobel Prize acceptance speech, Oslo, 1995. © 1995 The Nobel Foundation. Reproduced with permission.

7 'The Nuclear Issue: Pugwash and the Bush Policies'. The 53rd Pugwash Conference on Science and World Affairs: Advancing Human Security – The Role of Technology and Politics. Reproduced by permission of the US Pugwash Group.

The author and publisher gratefully acknowledge the copyright holders acknowledged above for permission to reproduce copyright material. The author and publisher apologize for any errors or omissions in the above list and would be grateful to be notified of any corrections that should be incorporated in the next edition or reprint of this book. The author and publisher are grateful to Jeffrey Boutwell, US Pugwash Group, for his assistance and advice on the Appendix section.

Appendix 1
'Leaving the Bomb'

A nuclear physicist responsible for helping design the atomic
bomb tells for the first time why he decided to leave
Los Alamos in 1944.

By Joseph Rotblat

*Joseph Rotblat is emeritus professor of physics at the University of London, St.
Bartholomew's Hospital Medical College. A founder of the Pugwash Conference
on Science and World Affairs, he was its secretary general for 17 years and is
currently chairman of the British Pugwash Group.*

Working on the Manhattan Project was a traumatic experience. It
is not often given to one to participate in the birth of a new era.
For some the effect has endured throughout their lives; I am one of those.

This essay is not an autobiography; it describes only my involvement
in the genesis of the atomic bomb. All extraneous personal elements are
left out, but their exclusion does not mean that they are unimportant.
Our hopes and fears, our resolutions and actions, are influenced by an
infinite number of small events interacting with each other all the time.
Because of this, each of us may react differently to the same set of conditions. The experience of every Los Alamite is unique.

At the beginning of 1939, when the news reached me of the discovery
of fission, I was working in the Radiological Laboratory in Warsaw.
Its director was Ludwik Wertenstein, a pupil of Marie Curie and a
pioneer in the science of radioactivity in Poland. Our source of radiation
consisted of 30 milligrams of radium in solution; every few days we
pumped the accumulated radon into a tube filled with beryllium
powder. With this minute neutron source we managed to carry out
much research, even competing with Enrico Fermi's prestigious team,
then in Rome, in the discovery of radionuclides. Our main achievement

was the direct evidence of the inelastic scattering of neutrons; my doctoral thesis was on that subject.

In the earlier experiments on inelastic scattering we used gold as the scatterer. By the end of 1938 I had begun to experiment with uranium, so when I heard of the fission of uranium, it did not take me long to set up an experiment to see whether neutrons are emitted as fission. I soon found that they are — indeed, that more neutrons are emitted than produce fission. From this discovery it was a fairly simple intellectual exercise to envisage a divergent chain reaction with a vast release of energy. The logical sequel was that if this energy were released in a very short time it would result in an explosion of unprecedented power. Many scientists in other countries, doing this type of research, went through a similar thought process, although not necessarily evoking the same reaction.

In my case, my first reflex was to put the whole thing out of my mind, like a person trying to ignore the first symptom of a fatal disease in the hope that it will go away. But the fear gnaws all the same, and my fear was that someone would put the idea into practice. The thought that I myself would do it did not cross my mind, because it was completely alien to me. I was brought up on humanitarian principles. At that time my life was centered on doing "pure" research work, but I always believed that science should be used in the service of mankind. The notion of utilizing my knowledge to produce an awesome weapon of destruction was abhorrent to me.

In my gnawing fear, the "someone" who might put it into practice was precisely defined: German scientists. I had no doubt that the Nazis would not hesitate to use any device, however inhumane, if it gave their doctrine world domination. If so, should one look into the problem to find out whether the fear had a realistic basis? Wrestling with this question was agonizing, and I was therefore glad that another pressing matter gave me an excuse to put it aside.

This other matter was my move to England, where I was to spend a year with Professor James Chadwick in Liverpool, on a grant to work on the cyclotron which was then being completed there. This was my first trip abroad, and the upheaval kept me busy both before the journey in April 1939 and for some time afterward, because I spoke very little English, and it took me a long time to settle down.

Throughout the spring and summer the gnawing went on relentlessly. It intensified with the increasing signs that Germany was getting ready for war. And it became acute when I read an article by S. Flügge in *Naturwissenschaften* mentioning the possibility of nuclear explosives.

Gradually I worked out a rationale for doing research on the feasibility of the bomb. I convinced myself that the only way to stop the Germans from using it against us would be if we too had the bomb and threatened to retaliate. My scenario never envisaged that we should use it, not even against the Germans. We needed the bomb for the sole purpose of making sure that it would not be used by the: the same argument that is now being used by proponents of the deterrence doctrine.

With the wisdom of hindsight, I can see the folly of the deterrent thesis, quite apart from a few other flaws in my rationalization. For one thing, it would not have worked with a psychopath like Hitler. If he had had the bomb, it is very likely that his last order from the bunker in Berlin would have been to destroy London, even if this were to bring terrible retribution to Germany. Indeed, he would have seen this as a heroic way of going down, in a *Götterdämmerung*.

My thinking at the time required that the feasibility of the atom bomb be established, one way or the other, with the utmost urgency. Yet I could not overcome my scruples. I felt the need to talk it over with someone, but my English was too halting to discuss such a sensitive issue with my colleagues in Liverpool.

In August 1939, having gone to Poland on a personal matter, I took the opportunity to visit Wertenstein and put my dilemma before him. The idea of a nuclear weapon had not occurred to him, but when I showed him my rough calculations he could not find anything scientifically wrong with them. On the moral issue, however, he was unwilling to advise me. He himself would never engage in this type of work, but he would not try to influence me. It had to be left to my own conscience.

The war broke out two days after I returned to Liverpool. Within a few weeks Poland was overrun. The stories that Hitler's military strength was all bluff, that his tanks were painted cardboard, turned out to be wishful thinking. The might of Germany stood revealed, and the whole of our civilization was in mortal peril. My scruples were finally overcome.

By November 1939 my English was good enough for me to give a course of lectures on nuclear physics to the Honors School at

Liverpool University, but by then the department's senior research staff had disappeared: they had gone to work on radar and other war projects. I had, therefore, to approach Chadwick directly with an outline of my plan for research on the feasibility of the atom bomb. His response was typically Chadwickian: he just grunted, without letting on whether he had already thought of such a plan. Later I learned that other scientists in the United Kingdom did have the same idea, some of them with similar motivation.

A few days later Chadwick told me to go ahead and gave me two young assistants. One of them presented a problem. He was a Quaker and as such had refused to do war work. He was therefore sent to Liverpool University for academic duties – but was diverted to work with me on the atom bomb! I was not allowed to reveal to him the nature of our research, and I had qualms of conscience about using him in such an unethical way.

The main idea which I put to Chadwick was that for the atom bomb the chain reaction would have to be propagated by fast neutrons; otherwise it would not differ much from a chemical explosive. It was therefore important to measure the fission cross-section for fast neutrons, the energy distribution of fission neutrons, their inelastic scattering, and the proportion of those captured without producing fission. It was also relevant to find out whether stray neutrons might cause a premature start of the reaction, which meant determining the probability of spontaneous fission of uranium.

We built up a small team of young but devoted physicists and used the cyclotron to tackle some of these problems. Later we were joined by Otto Frisch who measured the fast neutron fission cross-section for uranium-235. I had the idea of using plutonium, but we had no means of making it.

As a result of these investigations, we were able to establish that the atom bomb was feasible from the scientific point of view. However, it also became clear that in order to make the bomb a vast technological effort would be required, far exceeding the manpower and industrial potential of wartime Britain. A top-level decision was reached to collaborate with the Americans. And so I found myself eventually in that "wondrous strange" place, Los Alamos.

In March 1944 I experienced a disagreeable shock. At that time I was living with the Chadwicks in their house on the Mesa, before moving later to the "Big House," the quarters for single scientists. General Leslie Groves, when visiting Los Alamos, frequently came to the Chadwicks for dinner and relaxed palaver. During one such conversation Groves said that, of course, the real purpose in making the bomb was to subdue the Soviets. (Whatever his exact words, his real meaning was clear.) Although I had no illusions about the Stalin regime – after all, it was his pact with Hitler that enabled the latter to invade Poland – I felt deeply the sense of betrayal of an ally. Remember, this was said at a time when thousands of Russians were dying every day on the Eastern Front, tying down the Germans and giving the Allies time to prepare for the landing on the continent of Europe. Until then I had thought that our work was to prevent a Nazi victory, and now I was told that the weapon we were preparing was intended for use against the people who were making extreme sacrifices for that very aim.

My concern about the purpose of our work gained substance from conversations with Niels Bohr. He used to come to my room at eight in the morning to listen to the BBC news bulletin. Like myself, he could not stand the U.S. bulletins which urged us every few seconds to purchase a certain laxative! I owned a special radio on which I could receive the BBC World Service. Sometimes Bohr stayed on and talked to me about the social and political implications of the discovery of nuclear energy and of his worry about the dire consequences of a nuclear arms race between East and West which he foresaw.

All this, and the growing evidence that the war in Europe would be over before the bomb project was completed, made my participation in it pointless. If it took the Americans such a long time, then my fear of the Germans being first was groundless. When it became evident, toward the end of 1944, that the Germans had abandoned their bomb project, the whole purpose of my being in Los Alamos ceased to be, and I asked for permission to leave and return to Britain.

Why did other scientists not make the same decision? Obviously, one would not expect General Groves to wind up the project as soon as Germany was defeated, but there were many scientists for whom the German factor was the main motivation. Why did they not quit when this factor ceased to be?

I was not allowed to discuss this issue with anybody after I declared my intention to leave Los Alamos, but earlier conversations, as well as much later ones, elicited several reasons.

The most frequent reason given was pure and simple scientific curiosity – the strong urge to find out whether the theoretical calculations and predictions would come true. These scientists felt that only after the test at Alamogordo should they enter into the debate about the use of the bomb.

Others were prepared to put the matter off even longer, persuaded by the argument that many American lives would be saved if the bomb brought a rapid end to the war with Japan. Only when peace was restored would they take a hand in efforts to ensure that the bomb would not be used again.

Still others, while agreeing that the project should have been stopped when the German factor ceased to operate, were not willing to take an individual stand because they feared it would adversely affect their future career.

The groups I have just described – scientists with a social conscience – were a minority in the scientific community. The majority were not bothered by moral scruples; they were quite content to leave it to others to decide how their work would be used. Much the same situation exists now in many countries in relation to work on military projects. But it is the morality issue at a time of war that perplexes and worries me most.

Recently I came across a document released under the Freedom of Information Act. It is a letter, dated May 25, 1943, from Robert Oppenheimer to Enrico Fermi, on the military use of radioactive materials, specifically, the poisoning of food with radioactive strontium. The Smyth Report mentions such use as a possible German threat, but Oppenheimer apparently though the idea worthy of consideration, and asked Fermi whether he could produce the strontium without letting too many people into the secret. He went on: "I think we should not attempt a plan unless we can poison food sufficient to kill a half a million men." I am sure that in peacetime these same scientists would have viewed such a plan as barbaric; they would not have contemplated it even for a moment. Yet during the war it was considered quite seriously and, I presume, abandoned only because it was technically infeasible.

After I told Chadwick that I wished to leave the project, he came back to me with very disturbing news. When he conveyed my wish to the intelligence chief at Los Alamos, he was shown a thick dossier on me with highly incriminating evidence. It boiled down to my being a spy: I had arranged with a contact in Santa Fe to return to England, and then to be flown to and parachuted onto the part of Poland held by the Soviets, in order to give them the secrets of the atom bomb. The trouble was that within this load of rubbish was a grain of truth. I did indeed meet and converse with a person during my trips to Santa Fe. It was for a purely altruistic purpose, nothing to do with the project, and I had Chadwick's permission for the visits. Nevertheless, it contravened a security regulation, and it made me vulnerable.

Fortunately for me, in their zeal the vigilant agents had included in their reports details of conversations with dates, which were quite easy to refute and to expose as complete fabrications. The chief of intelligence was rather embarrassed by all this and conceded that the dossier was worthless. Nevertheless, he insisted that I not talk to anybody about my reason for leaving the project. We agreed with Chadwick that the ostensible reason would be a purely personal one: that I was worried about my wife whom I had left in Poland.

And so, on Christmas Eve 1944, I sailed for the United Kingdom, but not without another incident. Before leaving Los Alamos I packed all my documents – research notes as well as correspondence and other records – in a box made for me by my assistant. En route I stayed for a few days with the Chadwicks in Washington. Chadwick personally helped me to put the box on the train to New York. But when I arrived there a few hours later, the box was missing. Nor, despite valiant efforts, was it ever recovered.

The work on the Manhattan Project, as I said at the outset, has had an enduring effect on my life. Indeed, it radically changed my scientific career and the carrying out of my obligations to society.

Work on the atom bomb convinced me that even pure research soon finds applications of one kind or another. If so, I wanted to decide myself how my work should be applied. I chose an aspect of nuclear physics which would definitely be beneficial to humanity: the application to medicine. Thus I completely changed the direction of my research and spent the rest of my academic career working in a medical college and hospital. While this gave me personal satisfaction, I was increasingly concerned about the political aspects of the development of nuclear weapons, particularly the hydrogen bomb, about which I knew from Los Alamos. Therefore, I devoted myself both to arousing the scientific community to the danger, and to educating the general public on these issues. I was instrumental in setting up the Atomic Scientists Association in the United Kingdom, and within its framework organized the Atom Train, a travelling exhibition which explained to the public the good and evil aspects of nuclear energy. Through these activities I came to collaborate with Bertrand Russell. This association led to the foundation of the Pugwash Conferences, where I met again with colleagues from the Manhattan Project, who were also concerned about the threat to mankind that has arisen partly from their work.

After 40 years one question keeps nagging me: have we learned enough not to repeat the mistakes we made then? I am not sure even about myself. Not being an absolute pacifist, I cannot guarantee that I would not behave in the same way, should a similar situation arise. Our concepts of morality seem to get thrown overboard once military action starts. It is, therefore, most important not to allow such a situation to develop. Our prime effort must concentrate on the prevention of nuclear war, because in such a war not only morality but the whole fabric of civilization would disappear. Eventually, however, we must aim at eliminating all kinds of war.

Appendix 2
The Russell–Einstein Manifesto

Issued in London, 9 July 1955

In the tragic situation which confronts humanity, we feel that scientists should assemble in conference to appraise the perils that have arisen as a result of the development of weapons of mass destruction, and to discuss a resolution in the spirit of the appended draft.

We are speaking on this occasion, not as members of this or that nation, continent, or creed, but as human beings, members of the species Man, whose continued existence is in doubt. The world is full of conflicts; and, overshadowing all minor conflicts, the titanic struggle between Communism and anti-Communism.

Almost everybody who is politically conscious has strong feelings about one or more of these issues; but we want you, if you can, to set aside such feelings and consider yourselves only as members of a biological species which has had a remarkable history, and whose disappearance none of us can desire.

We shall try to say no single word which should appeal to one group rather than to another. All, equally, are in peril, and, if the peril is understood, there is hope that they may collectively avert it.

We have to learn to think in a new way. We have to learn to ask ourselves, not what steps can be taken to give military victory to whatever group we prefer, for there no longer are such steps; the question we have to ask ourselves is: what steps can be taken to prevent a military contest of which the issue must be disastrous to all parties?

The general public, and even many men in positions of authority, have not realized what would be involved in a war with nuclear bombs. The general public still thinks in terms of the obliteration of cities. It is understood that the new bombs are more powerful than the old, and that, while one A-bomb could obliterate Hiroshima, one H-bomb could obliterate the largest cities, such as London, New York, and Moscow.

No doubt in an H-bomb war great cities would be obliterated. But this is one of the minor disasters that would have to be faced. If everybody in London, New York, and Moscow were exterminated, the world might, in the course of a few centuries, recover from the blow. But we now know, especially since the Bikini test, that nuclear bombs can gradually spread destruction over a very much wider area than had been supposed.

It is stated on very good authority that a bomb can now be manufactured which will be 2,500 times as powerful as that which destroyed Hiroshima. Such a bomb, if exploded near the ground or under water, sends radio-active particles into the upper air. They sink gradually and reach the surface of the earth in the form of a deadly dust or rain. It was this dust which infected the Japanese fishermen and their catch of fish.

No one knows how widely such lethal radio-active particles might be diffused, but the best authorities are unanimous in saying that a war with H-bombs might possibly put an end to the human race. It is feared that if many H-bombs are used there will be universal death, sudden only for a minority, but for the majority a slow torture of disease and disintegration.

Many warnings have been uttered by eminent men of science and by authorities in military strategy. None of them will say that the worst results are certain. What they do say is that these results are possible, and no one can be sure that they will not be realized. We have not yet found that the views of experts on this question depend in any degree upon their politics or prejudices. They depend only, so far as our researches have revealed, upon the extent of the particular expert's knowledge. We have found that the men who know most are the most gloomy.

Here, then, is the problem which we present to you, stark and dreadful and inescapable: Shall we put an end to the human race; or shall mankind renounce war? People will not face this alternative because it is so difficult to abolish war.

The abolition of war will demand distasteful limitations of national sovereignty. But what perhaps impedes understanding of the situation more than anything else is that the term "mankind" feels vague and abstract. People scarcely realize in imagination that the danger is to themselves and their children and their grandchildren, and not only to a dimly apprehended humanity. They can scarcely bring themselves to grasp that they, individually, and those whom they love are in imminent danger of perishing agonizingly. And so they hope that perhaps war may be allowed to continue provided modern weapons are prohibited.

This hope is illusory. Whatever agreements not to use H-bombs had been reached in time of peace, they would no longer be considered binding in time of war, and both sides would set to work to manufacture H-bombs as soon as war broke out, for, if one side manufactured the bombs and the other did not, the side that manufactured them would inevitably be victorious.

Although an agreement to renounce nuclear weapons as part of a general reduction of armaments would not afford an ultimate solution, it would serve certain important purposes. First: any agreement between East and West is to the good in so far as it tends to diminish tension. Second: the abolition of thermo-nuclear weapons, if each side believed that the other had carried it out sincerely, would lessen the fear of a sudden attack in the style of Pearl Harbour, which at present keeps both sides in a state of nervous apprehension. We should, therefore, welcome such an agreement though only as a first step.

Most of us are not neutral in feeling, but, as human beings, we have to remember that, if the issues between East and West are to be decided in any manner that can give any possible satisfaction to anybody, whether Communist or anti-Communist, whether Asian or European or American, whether White or Black, then these issues must not be decided by war. We should wish this to be understood, both in the East and in the West.

There lies before us, if we choose, continual progress in happiness, knowledge, and wisdom. Shall we, instead, choose death, because we cannot forget our quarrels? We appeal, as human beings, to human beings: Remember your humanity, and forget the rest. If you can do so, the way lies open to a new Paradise; if you cannot, there lies before you the risk of universal death.

Resolution
We invite this Congress, and through it the scientists of
The world and the general public, to subscribe to
The following resolution:

"In view of the fact that in any future world war nuclear weapons will certainly be employed, and that such weapons threaten the continued existence of mankind, we urge the Governments of the world to realize, and to acknowledge publicly, that their purpose cannot be furthered by a world war, and we urge them, consequently, to find peaceful means for the settlement of all matters of dispute between them."

Max Born
Perry W. Bridgman
Albert Einstein
Leopold Infeld
Frédéric Joliot-Curie
Herman J. Muller
Linus Pauling
Cecil F. Powell
Joseph Rotblat
Bertrand Russell
Hideki Yukawa

Appendix 3

Statement from the First Pugwash Conference, held in Pugwash, July, 7–10, 1957

At the invitation of Lord Russell, and through the generous hospitality of Mr. Cyrus Eaton, a group of scientists, drawn from ten nations and widely representative of different political, economic and other opinions, met in Conference at Pugwash, Nova Scotia, between July 7 and 10, 1957. Mr. Y. Shimonaka and others also provided valuable assistance.

The meeting originated in the suggestion contained in the Russell–Einstein appeal, that scientists should meet to assess the perils to humanity which have arisen as a result of the development of weapons of mass destruction. Two years have passed since that statement was issued but the dangers remain. In fact, the stockpiles of nuclear weapons have increased, new nations have joined the ranks of those producing weapons, or trying to produce them, whilst serious misgivings have been expressed as to whether the continued testing of such weapons may not result in damage to the population. The general belief that a full-scale nuclear war would bring universal disaster upon mankind, and the recognition that it is technically possible for both the two great contending forces to visit any desired degree of destruction upon an enemy, as well as certain political developments, have created an atmosphere in which it was possible for us to meet, and to discuss dispassionately, many important and highly controversial issues.

The international problems which have arisen as a result of the development of atomic energy are of two kinds, technical and political. A gathering of men of science can discuss with special competence only the scientific and technical implications of atomic energy. Such discussion, however, can be fruitful only if it takes into account the political problems which are the background to international negotiations. The signatories of the Russell–Einstein appeal affirmed their intention to say nothing which might seem to favour one rather than the other of the two great groups of powers into which the world is divided. In attempting to formulate the conclusions which followed from our discussions, we too have tried to avoid any exacerbation of the differences between nations which might follow, for example, from emphasis on technical considerations unwelcome to one or other of the two great powers.

Men of science are now well aware that the fruits of their labours are of paramount importance for the future of mankind, and they are thus compelled to consider the political implications of their work. Their opinions on politics are as diverse as those of other men. These facts make it difficult for a conference such as the present to issue an agreed statement on matters which are controversial. The discussion of such issues, however, allowed the points of difference and the areas of agreement to be defined, and led to a measure of mutual understanding of the opinions of one another.

The main work of the meeting was centered around three principal topics: (1) the hazards arising from the use of atomic energy in peace and war; (2) problems of the control of nuclear weapons; and (3) the social responsibility of scientists. Three committees were established to give detailed consideration to these topics. Their reports to the conference are given in the statements appended to this document, but the principal conclusions bearing on the hazards of atomic energy may be briefly summarized as follows:

Committee I, on nuclear hazards, made an independent assessment of the effects of the nuclear tests carried out hitherto. From the details given in the appendix, it may be seen that the hazard, compared with others to which mankind is subject from natural causes, is small. Nevertheless, because of the world-wide distribution of fission products, and the fact that some areas may be subject to effects much above the average, close attention to the dangers should be maintained, especially if tests of bombs which give large radioactive fall-out continue to be made.

The committee also considered the hazards arising from the peacetime use of industrial atomic power, or the application of radiations in medicine and industry. Although these hazards must be viewed in the light of the great benefits which will flow from such applications, means of greatly reducing the attendant hazards are available and should be widely adopted.

The above-mentioned estimates of the hazards which have arisen from test explosions, permitted a closer examination to be made of the probable consequences of an unrestricted nuclear war. This examination led to the unquestioned conclusion that a general war with nuclear weapons would indeed represent a disaster of unprecedented magnitude. The radiological hazards would be thousands of times greater than those due to the fall-out effects of test explosions. In the combatant countries, hundreds of millions of people would be killed outright by the blast and heat, and by the ionizing radiation produced at the instant of explosion whether bombs of the so-called "clean" or "dirty" kind were employed. If "dirty" bombs were used, large areas would be made uninhabitable for extended periods of time, and additional hundreds of millions of people would die from delayed effects of radiation from local fall-out, some in the exposed population from direct radiation injury, and some in succeeding generations as a result of genetic effects. But even countries not directly hit by bombs would suffer through global fall-out, which, under certain conditions, might be of such intensity as to cause large-scale genetic and other injury.

It is against the background of the fearful consequences for humanity of a general war with nuclear weapons that the conclusions of Committee II, which considered problems of control, must be viewed. The principal objective of all nations must be the abolition of war and the threat of war hanging over mankind. War must be finally eliminated, not merely regulated by limiting the weapons which may be used. For this purpose, it is necessary to reduce tension among the nations; to promote mutual understanding among the people; to strive for the ending of the arms race; and to provide an adequate control system so as to give substantial protection, and permit the development of mutual confidence.

One of the greatest difficulties in international affairs in recent years has sprung from the fact that in a period of delicate strategic balance, even secondary questions acquire strategic significance; in such a situation, they are rarely subject to agreed solutions because any particular solution appears to be to the strategic advantage of one rather than another of the powers. We believe that it is unrealistic to depend upon any sudden increase in mutual confidence and that it is more likely to grow from small beginnings. In this situation, even small agreements covering limited fields could be of great importance.

In the present circumstances, we believe that the greatest peril comes from the possibility that a war might break out between two smaller nations, that Russia and America might intervene militarily on opposite sides, and that such a war might be fought by using atomic bombs in combat. We believe it would be very difficult to limit a local war of this kind – particularly if it is fought with atomic weapons in the tactical area – and that what may start out as a local war may end as a general atomic catastrophe. In order to avert this danger, political settlements aimed specifically at eliminating the risk of the outbreak of a local war between smaller nations are needed.

The conclusions of Committee III on the responsibilities of scientists state our common conviction that we should do all in our power to prevent war and to assist in establishing a permanent and universal peace. This we can do by contributing to the task of public enlightenment concerning the great dilemma of our times; and by serving to the full extent of our opportunities in the formation of national policies. The committee gives a statement of beliefs and aspirations suitable for scientists in the modern world.

Finally, we should like to give expression to the high degree of unanimity we have found among all the members of the conference on *fundamental aims*. We are all convinced that mankind must abolish war or suffer catastrophe; that the dilemma of opposing power groups and the arms race must be broken; and that the establishment of lasting peace will mark the opening of a new and triumphant epoch for the whole of mankind. We earnestly hope that our conference may make a modest contribution to these great aims.

Report of Committee I

Radiation Hazards

The effects of radiation, from nuclear tests, from peaceful applications, and from the possible wartime use of nuclear weapons, have been the subject of much concern and study. We have felt it desirable at this meeting to consider the available facts bearing on these problems.

With regard to the effects of nuclear testing we have found that separate calculations carried out independently in Great Britain, Japan, the

U.S.A. and the U.S.S.R. have yielded results in good agreement with one another on the amount of fallout and on its effects.

A principal effect is due to strontium-90. If, as some evidence indicates, the production of leukaemia and bone cancer by radiation is proportional to the dose, even down to very small doses, then we estimate that the tests conducted over the past six years will be responsible for an increase of about 1 per cent over the natural incidence of leukaemia and bone cancer during the next few decades. Over the next 30 years, this increase would amount to about a hundred thousand additional cases of leukaemia and bone cancer. The correct numbers may be several times larger or smaller. These additional cases could, however, not be identified among the 10 million or so normal cases of the same diseases.

A second principal effect of global fallout consists of genetic mutations. We estimate that these will cause serious injury to about as many individuals as those in whom leukaemia or bone cancer will be produced by the strontium-90. However, the genetic effects from a given amount of fallout, unlike the effects of strontium-90 will be scattered over many generations.

Peacetime uses of radiation, such as x-rays in medicine, or nuclear power production, will also be responsible for the delivery of radiation to large numbers of people. Genetic and long-term somatic effects will result from this radiation, in amounts depending on how much radiation is received by the reproductive cells and by other parts of the body.

It is important, in evaluating the effects from various sources of radiation, to try to put them in proper perspective. For example, the radiation received by the average individual from medical x-rays, is, in countries of more highly-developed techniques, considerably greater than the fallout radiation from tests at the recent rate. This does not mean, however, either that we should stop using x-rays, or that we should not be concerned about fallout from tests. Great benefits to man are obtained from the use of x-rays, as well as from the industrial use of nuclear energy. The new awareness concerning the deleterious effects of radiation is leading to greatly improved techniques in the use of x-rays, and to more rigorous precaution in the application of nuclear energy. By these means it will be possible to reduce the doses received from medical and industrial radiation to levels that are justifiable in the light of the benefits obtained. It is useful to remember that modern industrialized society involves many developments with harmful side effects, as in the case, for example, of the fumes from automobiles and from industrial establishments. Accurate evaluation of the damage caused in this way has not been made but, even if it should turn out to be considerable, no one would expect to stop using all automobile engines or noxious industrial processes.

With regard to fallout effects from tests, it should be recognized that the effects are global, and exerted upon citizens of all countries, regardless of whether they or their governments have approved the holding of tests. In these circumstances, the usual criteria as to whether a given hazard is justifiable cannot be applied. According to the figures given above, many individuals will be affected, although the numbers represent only a small percentage increase over normally occurring effects, and it will not be possible to say, for example, which specific case of leukaemia is due to fallout and which is a natural case. It should also be realized that appreciable areas of the world will experience higher than average effects from fallout.

We now come to the consideration of the effects of a nuclear war. It cannot be disputed that a full-scale nuclear war would be an utter catastrophe. Its effects would be thousands of times greater than the fallout effects from nuclear tests. In the combatant countries, hundreds of millions of people would be killed outright, by the flash and heat, and by the ionizing radiation produced at the instant of explosion. If so-called "dirty" bombs were used, large areas would be made uninhabitable for extended periods of time, and additional hundreds of millions of people would probably die from delayed effects of local fallout radiation; some in the exposed population from direct radiation injury and some in succeeding generations as a result of genetic effects. Even countries not directly hit by bombs would suffer through global fallout, which under certain conditions might be of such intensity as to cause large-scale genetic and other injury.

Report of Committee II

In this age of atomic weapons, the objective of all nations must be the abolition of war and even the threat of war from the life of mankind. War must be eliminated, not merely regulated by limiting the weapons to be used. The advancement of this objective calls for:

1. The lessening of tensions among nations and the promotion of mutual understanding among their peoples.

2. The ending of the arms race.

3. The provision of reasonable safeguards in the arms control system to give substantial protection and build up mutual confidence. The development of atomic armaments has now gone so far that a completely effective and reliable control system appears to be no longer possible.

4. The initiation of a step-by-step process to develop as satisfactory a set of controls and safeguards as practicable. The prompt suspension of nuclear bomb tests could be a good first step for this purpose.

Report of Committee III

It is our conviction that the paramount responsibility of scientists outside their professional work is to do all in their power to prevent war and to help establish a permanent and universal peace. This they can do by contributing to the full measure of their capabilities to public enlightenment on the destructive and constructive potentialities of science and by contributing to the full extent of their opportunities in the formation of national policies.

To this aim, scientists of all countries without regard to political and economic systems can dedicate themselves because they share certain common beliefs. Following are some of them:

1. With the penetration of science into the world of atomic nuclei, humanity has entered a new epoch.

2. The development of science and technology has paramount importance for the future of all mankind. This imposes upon scientists the obligation to be more actively concerned with matters of public policy, and upon political leaders the duty to take fully into account the scientific and technological facts.

3. As a consequence of man's mastery of nuclear forces, a war can now cause immeasurable damage to mankind.

4. If the achievements of science are rationally employed, they could enormously increase the well-being of all men.

5. Scientific and technical progress is irreversible. With humanity basing much of its technological progress on the manipulation of nuclear

forces, it is of paramount importance that war be made permanently and universally impossible.

6. In the past, nations have often resorted to force in the quest for natural resources and fruits of labour. These methods must now be replaced by a common effort to create wealth for all.

7. The security of mankind demands that no section of it shall have the capacity to destroy the other. The developments of science and technology tend to break down barriers between nations and, in effect, to unify mankind.

8. The need of all parts of mankind to co-operate in the growth of the total sum of human knowledge and wealth, despite ideological and other differences which may divide them, is permanent and not a matter of temporary "co-existence" of different political or economic systems.

9. Tradition tends to place the emphasis in the education of youth on separate ideals of single nations, including the glorification of wars. The atomic age urgently requires a modification of these traditions. Without abandoning loyalty to national heritage or fundamental principles of the different societies, education must emphasize the fundamental and permanent community of the interests of mankind, in peace and co-operation, irrespective of national boundaries and differences in economic or political systems.

10. Science has a well proven tradition of international co-operation. We hope that this co-operation can be strengthened and extended into other fields of human endeavour.

11. Science develops most effectively when it is free from interference by any dogma imposed from the outside, and permitted to question all postulates, including her own. Without this freedom of scientific thought and the freedom to exchange information and ideas, full utilization of the constructive possibilities of science will not be possible.

Participants

Australia	Prof. M. L. E. Oliphant
Austria	Prof. H. Thirring
Canada	Dr. G. Brock Chisholm
	Prof. J. S. Foster
China	Prof. Chou Pei Yuan
France	Prof. A. M. B. Lacassagne

Japan	Prof. I. Ogawa
	Prof. S. Tomonaga
	Prof. H. Yukawa
Poland	Prof. M. Danysz
U.K.	Prof. C. F. Powell
	Prof. J. Rotblat
U.S.A.	Prof. D. F. Cavers
	Prof. P. Doty
	Prof. H. J. Muller
	Prof. E. Rabinowitch
	P of. W. Selve
	Prof. L. Szilard
	Prof. V. Weisskopf

Appendix 4

Statement from the Third Pugwash Conference, held in Kitzbühel and Vienna, September 14–20, 1958

VIENNA DECLARATION

1. *Necessity to End Wars*

We meet in Kitzbühel and in Vienna at a time when it has become evident that the development of nuclear weapons makes it possible for man to destroy civilization and, indeed, himself; the means of destruction are being made ever more efficient. The scientists attending our meetings have long been concerned with this development, and they are unanimous in the opinion that a full-scale nuclear war would be a world-wide catastrophe of unprecedented magnitude.

In our opinion defence against nuclear attack is very difficult. Unfounded faith in defensive measures may even contribute to an outbreak of war.

Although the nations may agree to eliminate nuclear weapons and other weapons of mass destruction from the arsenals of the world, the knowledge of how to produce such weapons can never be destroyed. They remain for all time a potential threat for mankind. In any future major war, each belligerent state will feel not only free but compelled to undertake immediate production of nuclear weapons; for no state, when at war, can be sure that such steps are not being taken by the enemy. We believe that, in such a situation, a major industrial power would require less than one year to begin accumulating weapons. From then on, the only restraint against their employment in war would be agreements not to use them, which were concluded in times of peace.

The decisive power of nuclear weapons, however, would make the temptation to use them almost irresistible, particularly to leaders who are facing defeat. It appears, therefore, that atomic weapons are likely to be employed in any future major war with all their terrible consequences.

It is sometimes suggested that localized wars, with limited objective, might still be fought without catastrophic consequences. History shows, however, that the risk of local conflicts growing into major wars is too great to be acceptable in the age of weapons of mass destruction. Mankind must, therefore, set itself the task of eliminating all wars, including local wars.

2. *Requirements for Ending the Arms Race*

The armaments race is the result of distrust between states; it also contributes to this distrust. Any step that mitigates the arms race, and leads to even small reductions in armaments and armed forces, on an equitable basis and subject to necessary control, is therefore desirable. We welcome all steps in this direction and, in particular, the recent agreement in Geneva between representatives of East and West about the feasibility of detecting test-explosions. As scientists, we take particular pleasure in the fact that this unanimous agreement, the first after a long series of unsuccessful international disarmament negotiations, was made possible by mutual understanding and a common objective approach by scientists from different countries. We note with satisfaction that the governments of the U.S.A., U.S.S.R., and U.K. have approved the statements and the conclusion contained in the report of the technical experts. This is a significant success; we most earnestly hope that this approval will soon be followed by an international agreement leading to the cessation of all nuclear weapon tests and an effective system of control. This would be a first step toward the relaxation of international tension and the end of the arms race.

It is generally agreed that any agreement on disarmament, and in particular nuclear disarmament, requires measures of control to protect every party from possible evasion. Through their technical competence, scientists are well aware that effective control will in some cases be relatively easy, while it is very difficult in others. For example, the conference of experts in Geneva has agreed that the cessation of bomb tests could be monitored by a suitable network of detecting stations. On the other hand, it will be a technical problem of great difficulty to account fully for existing stocks of nuclear weapons and other means of mass destruction. An agreement to cease production of nuclear weapons presents a problem of intermediate technical difficulty between these two extreme examples.

We recognize that the accumulation of large stocks of nuclear weapons has made a completely reliable system of controls for far-reaching nuclear disarmament extremely difficult, perhaps impossible. For this disarmament to become possible, nations may have to depend, in addition to a practical degree of technical verification, on a combination of political agreements, of successful international security arrangements, and of experience of successful co-operation in various areas. Together, these can create the climate of mutual trust, which does not now exist, and an assurance that nations recognize the mutual political advantages of avoiding suspicion.

Recognizing the difficulties of the technological situation, scientists feel an obligation to impress on their peoples and on their governments the need for policies which will encourage international trust and reduce mutual apprehension. Mutual apprehensions cannot be reduced by assertions of good will; their reduction will require political adjustment and the establishment of active co-operation.

3. *What War Would Mean*

Our conclusions about the possible consequences of war have been supported by reports and papers submitted to our Conference. These documents indicate that if, in a future war, a substantial proportion of the nuclear weapons already manufactured were delivered against urban targets, most centres of civilization in the belligerent countries would be totally destroyed, and most of their populations killed. This would be true whether the bombs used derived most of their power from fusion reactions (so-called "clean" bombs) or principally from fission reactions (so-called "dirty" bombs). In addition to destroying major centres of population and industry, such bombs would also wreck the economy of the country attacked, through the destruction of vital means of distribution and communication.

Major states have already accumulated large stocks of "dirty" nuclear weapons; it appears that they are continuing to do so. From a strictly military point of view, dirty bombs have advantages in some situations; this makes likely their use in a major war.

The local fallout resulting from extensive use of "dirty" bombs would cause the death of a large part of the population in the country attacked. Following their explosion in large numbers (each explosion equivalent to that of millions of tons of ordinary chemical explosive), radioactive fallout would be distributed, not only over the territory to which they were delivered but, in varying intensity, over the rest of the earth's surface. Many millions of deaths would thus be produced, not only in belligerent but also in non-belligerent countries, by the acute effects of radiation.

There would be, further, substantial long-term radiation damage, to human and other organisms everywhere, from somatic effects such as leukaemia, bone cancer, and shortening of the life span; and from genetic damage affecting the hereditary traits transmitted to the progeny.

Knowledge of human genetics is not yet sufficient to allow precise predictions of consequences likely to arise from the considerable increase in the rate of mutation which would ensue from unrestricted nuclear war. However, geneticists believe that they may well be serious for the future of a surviving world population.

It is sometimes suggested that in a future war, the use of nuclear weapons might be restricted to objectives such as military bases, troop concentrations, airfields, and other communication centres; and that attacks on large centres of population could thus be avoided.

Even tactical weapons now have a large radius of action; cities and towns are commonly closely associated with centres of supply and transportation. We, therefore, believe that even a "restricted" war would lead, despite attempted limitation of targets, to widespread devastation of the territory in which it took place, and to the destruction of much of its population. Further, an agreement not to use cities for military purposes, entered into in order to justify their immunity from attack, is unlikely to be maintained to the end of a war, particularly by the losing side. The latter would also be strongly tempted to use nuclear bombs against the population centres of the enemy, in the hope of breaking his will to continue the war.

4. *Hazards of Bomb Tests*

At our first conference it had been agreed that while the biological hazards of bomb tests may be small compared with similar hazards to which mankind is exposed from other sources, hazards from tests exist and should receive close and continual study. Since then, an extensive investigation by the United Nations Scientific Committee on the Effects of Atomic Radiation has been carried out and its authoritative conclusions published. In this case, too, scientists from many different countries have been able to arrive at a unanimous agreement. Their conclusions confirm that the bomb tests produce a definite hazard and that they will claim a significant number of victims in present and following generations. Though the magnitude of the genetic damage appears to be relatively small compared with that produced by natural causes, the incidence of leukaemia and bone cancer due to the radioactivity from test explosions may, in the estimate of the U.N. committee, add significantly to the natural incidence of these diseases. This conclusion depends on the assumption (not shared by all authorities in the field) that these effects can be produced even by the smallest amount of radiation. This uncertainty calls for extensive study and, in the meantime, for a prudent acceptance of the most pessimistic assumption. It lends emphasis to the generally agreed conclusion that all unnecessary exposure of mankind to radiation is undesirable and should be avoided.

It goes without saying that the biological damage from a war, in which many nuclear bombs would be used, would be incomparably larger than that from tests; the main immediate problem before mankind is thus the establishment of conditions that would eliminate war.

5. *Science and International Co-operation*

We believe that, as scientists, we have an important contribution to make toward establishing trust and co-operation among nations. Science is, by long tradition, an international undertaking. Scientists with different national allegiances easily find a common basis of understanding; they use the same concepts and the same methods; they work toward common intellectual goals, despite differences in philosophical, economic, or political views. The rapidly growing importance of science of the affairs of mankind increases the importance of the community of understanding.

The ability of scientists all over the world to understand one another, and to work together, is an excellent instrument for bridging the gap between nations and for uniting them around common aims. We believe that working together in every field where international co-operation proves possible makes an important contribution toward establishing an appreciation of the community of nations. It can contribute to the development of the climate of mutual trust, which is necessary for the resolution of political conflicts between nations, and which is an essential background to effective disarmament. We hope scientists everywhere will recognize their responsibility, to mankind and to their own nations, to contribute thought, time, and energy to the furthering of international co-operation.

Several international scientific undertakings have already had considerable success. We mention only the century-old, world wide co-operation in weather science, the two International Polar Years which preceded (by seventy-five and twenty-five years respectively), the present International Geophysical Year, and the Atoms-for-Peace Conferences. We earnestly hope that efforts will be made to initiate similar collaboration in other fields of study. Certainly they will have the enthusiastic support of scientists all over the world.

We call for an increase in the unrestricted flow of scientific information among nations, and for a wide exchange of scientists. We believe that nations which build their national security on secrecy of scientific developments sacrifice the interests of peace, and of the progress of science, for temporary advantages. It is our belief that science can best serve mankind if it is free from interference by any dogma imposed from outside, and if it exercises its right to question all postulates, including its own.

6. *Technology in the Service of Peace*

In our time, pure and applied sciences have become increasingly interdependent. The achievements of fundamental, experimental and theoretical science are more and more rapidly transformed into new technological developments. This accelerated trend is manifest, alike in the creation of weapons of increased destructiveness, and in the development of means for the increased wealth and well-being of mankind. We believe that the tradition of mutual understanding and of international co-operation, which have long existed in fundamental science, can and should be extended to many fields of technology. The International Atomic Energy Agency, for example, aims not merely at co-operation for establishing facts about atomic energy, but also at helping the nations of the world to develop a new source of energy as a basis for the improvement of their material welfare. We believe that international co-operation in this and other fields, such as economic development and the promotion of health, should be greatly strengthened.

The extremely low level of living in the industrially underdeveloped countries of the world is and will remain a source of international tension. We see an urgent need to forward studies and programmes for the effective industrialization of these countries. This would not only improve the level of living of the majority of the population of the world; it would also help to reduce the sources of conflict between the highly industrialized powers. Such studies would offer fruitful scope for co-operative efforts between scientists of all nations.

The great increase in the ease and speed of communications, and our increasing understanding of how the forces of nature influence the living conditions of nations in different parts of the world, show us, in a way not previously possible, the extent to which the prosperity of individual nations is connected with, and dependent upon, that of mankind as a whole; and how rapidly it could be increased by common international effort. We believe that through such common effort, the co-existence between nations of different social and economic structure can become not merely peaceful and competitive, but to an increasing degree co-operative, and therefore more stable.

As scientists, we are deeply aware of the great change in the condition of mankind which has been brought about by the modern development and application of science. Given peace, mankind stands at the beginning of a great scientific age. Science can provide mankind with an ever increasing understanding of the forces of nature and the means of harnessing them. This will bring about a great increase in the well-being, health, and prosperity of all men.

7. *The Responsibility of Scientists*

We believe it to be a responsibility of scientists in all countries to contribute to the education of the peoples by spreading among them a wide understanding of the dangers and potentialities offered by the unprecedented growth of science. We appeal to our colleagues everywhere to contribute to this effort, both through enlightenment of adult populations, and through education of the coming generations. In particular, education should stress improvement of all forms of human relations and should eliminate any glorification of war and violence.

Scientists are, because of their special knowledge, well equipped for early awareness of the danger and the promise arising from scientific discoveries. Hence, they have a special competence and a special responsibility in relation to the most pressing problems of our times.

In the present conditions of distrust between nations, and of the race for military supremacy which arises from it, all branches of science – physics, chemistry, biology, psychology – have become increasingly involved in military developments. In the eyes of the people of many countries, science has become associated with the development of weapons. Scientists are either admired for their contribution to national security, or damned for having brought mankind into jeopardy by their invention of weapons of mass destruction. The increasing material support which science now enjoys in many countries is mainly due to its importance, direct or indirect, to the military strength of the nation and to its degree of success in the arms race. This diverts science from its true purpose, which is to increase human knowledge, and to promote man's mastery over the forces of nature for the benefit of all.

We deplore the conditions which lead to this situation, and appeal to all peoples and their governments to establish conditions of lasting and stable peace.

Participants

Australia	Prof. M. L. E. Oliphant
Austria	Prof. Hans Thirring
Bulgaria	Acad. G. Nadjakov
Canada	Dr. Brock Chisholm
	Sir Robert Watson-Watt

Czechoslovakia	Dr. Viktor Knap
	Dr. J. Kozesník
Denmark	Prof. Mogens Pihl
Federal German Republic	Prof. Max Born
	Prof. G. Burkhardt
	Prof. Helmut Hönl
	Prof. Werner Kliefoth
	Dr. Hanfried Lenz
France	Father Pierre-Leon Dubarle
	Dr. Bernard Gregory
	Dr. J. Gueron
	Prof. Antoine Lacassagne
German Democratic Republic	Prof. Günther Rienäcker
Hungary	Prof. Lajos Janossy
India	Dr. H. J. Bhabha
	Sir K. S. Krishnan
	Prof. P. C. Mahalanobis

Appendix 5

Proceedings of the Forty-Second Pugwash Conference on Science and World Affairs

Berlin, Germany, 11–17 September, 1992

Shaping our Common Future: Dangers and Opportunities

TIME TO RETHINK THE IDEA OF WORLD GOVERNMENT

Closing Address by *Joseph Rotblat*

At this Quinquennial Conference we have adopted the Pugwash goals for the next five years. The discussion this morning elucidated some further specific and general tasks for Pugwash. In this closing address I want to advance ideas, which, I believe, are essential to the achievement of our ultimate goal, the elimination of all war, ideas which the polite among you may say are very ambitious, and others will call Utopian. What I have in mind – and I will spell it out straight away – is the idea of a Federal World Government.

The tremendous changes in the recent years have proved that nothing is beyond achievement in the world of politics: what was unimaginable yesterday is reality today; and what is Utopian today may be the actuality of tomorrow. May be, but it will not happen tomorrow if we shy away from talking about it today.

Both our founding fathers, Albert Einstein and Bertrand Russell, were strong advocates of a World Government, even though this was not spelled out in the Manifesto. In the Manifesto they elucidated the alternatives facing mankind:

"Here, then, is the problem which we present to you, stark and dreadful and inescapable: Shall we put an end to the human race; or shall mankind renounce war?"

and they pointed out the requirement for the latter alternative:

"The abolition of war will demand distasteful limitations of national sovereignty."

But the Manifesto stopped short of calling for a world government, because there was no chance of it being agreed to by some signatories of the Manifesto, notably Frederic Joliot-Curie. The communists were implacable opponents of a world government.

But now we are living in a different world.

At the opening session of this Conference, I said that the significance of the events that have occurred since the Beijing conference a year ago, namely, the disintegration of the Soviet Union and the demise of the Communist regime there, has not yet fully penetrated the minds of people. For most of this century we lived in a bipolar world, dominated by an ideological division, and described in the Russell–Einstein Manifesto as:

"The titanic struggle between Communism and anti-Communism."

It is very difficult to adapt oneself mentally to the new political configuration in which erstwhile mortal enemies have become, in the words of Boris Yeltsin, 'friends and partners'.

This slow adaptation to the new situation is chiefly due to inertia: most people hate change; it is painful to abandon old beliefs, to accept new precepts. And this natural conservatism is reinforced by groups with vested interests, by people whose careers, or huge profits, are founded on the old concepts that kept the world divided and at war, concepts based on secrecy which fuels suspicion the mistrust. These concepts are just the opposite to those which, I am sure, most of you share with me, namely, *oneness and openness*. It was these concepts that scientists attempted to promote at the advent of the nuclear age, when the atom bomb was being made.

From the very beginning, nuclear weapons were seen by many politicians and military leaders in the United States, as the major tool for waging the ideological war. The atom bomb was developed during World War II, not to deter Hitler from using it against the Allies – as many of those who initiated the work on the bomb believed – but to subdue the Soviets. And the Soviets, in turn, developed it to deny the Americans absolute superiority. And so we found ourselves engaged in an insane arms race, which, had it continued, would have inevitably resulted in a nuclear confrontation and, very likely, in the end of civilization.

This was foreseen by scientists very early, especially by Niels Bohr, who already in 1944 predicted with prophetic vision the dire consequences of a nuclear arms race. The basic principle of Bohr's philosophy was openness. In science openness is of course a *sine qua non*, but Bohr advocated its extension to the realm of politics, to problems of security. He said:

" . . . *it must be realized that full mutual openness, only, can effectively promote confidence and guarantee common security.*"

Bohr's proposals were rejected, but after Hiroshima and Nagasaki, other scientists made an attempt to prevent future such horror: foremost among them was Eugene Rabinowitch, a spiritual leader of Pugwash. Earlier, the Franck Report, of which he was the main author, said:

"*Among all the arguments calling for an efficient international organization for peace, the existence of nuclear weapons is the most compelling one.*"

The Franck Report was the inspiration for the Acheson–Lilienthal Report, which advocated strict international control of nuclear weapons. Under the heading:

"*Disclosure of information as an essential of international action.*"

and following Bohr's philosophy, it stated:

"*We believe that this is the firmest basis of security: for in the long-term there can be no international control and no international cooperation which does not presuppose an international community of knowledge.*"

All this talk about openness was anathema to General Groves, the head of the Manhattan Project, but after the devastation of the Japanese cities the revulsion against the bomb was so great that nobody dared to come out openly against such a proposal; indeed, General Groves himself signed the Acheson-Lilienthal Report. However, in the end the hawks had their way. When the ideas of the scientists were formulated in the official proposals of the United States to the United Nations – the famous (or, some will say, notorious) Baruch Plan – significant changes had been made to them to ensure that the Plan would not be accepted by the Soviets. This was what in fact happened. We are all painfully familiar with the consequences of that failure of the ideas of the scientists.

It was a stroke of luck that a visionary man took over the leadership of the Soviet Union at a critical moment. Mikhail Gorbachev adopted the new way of thinking which we have always advocated in Pugwash; he revived the concepts on which the early proposals of scientists were based in relation to security. In his book *Perestroika* he said:

"The new political outlook calls for the recognition of one more simple axiom: security is indivisible. It is either equal security for all or none at all . . . The security of each nation should be coupled with the security of all members of the world community . . . Consequently, there should be no striving for security for oneself at the expense of others."

In order to sell these ideas to his own people, Gorbachev had to advance openness; he introduced *glasnost*. By doing this he unlocked the floodgates, and eventually he himself was engulfed in the flood. The finale was dramatic: the 75-year ideological struggle was over.

However, the very removal of the oppressive communist regime has given birth to a new source of conflict and military confrontation, the splitting of nations. The drive for independence by various entities is of long standing, but the collapse of the Soviet Union gave it renewed impetus. Should this trend continue, we may end up with a hundred nations in Europe alone, but it is very doubtful whether under the present world political system this would lead to stability.

One of the problems is that ethnicity can no longer be directly related to territory, as the tragic case of Bosnia is demonstrating. The perpetual conflict arising from this source, and from the refusal of states to grant independence to their minority groups, is present even in long-established nations, and the problem has become acute after the recent changes in the political configuration.

In my opinion there can be no lasting solution to it as long as the present concept of the nation-state persists; and this concept is bound to persist as long as the world political system is based on the present Charter of the United Nations.

The basic principle of the United Nations is the sovereignty of all its members. The Charter forbids the United Nations to intervene in matters that are within the domestic jurisdiction of any state. The world community of nations is called upon to defend the territorial integrity of every member-state, but is prohibited from interceding in internal affairs of a state, even if that state carries out heinous crimes against its own people.

People of good will – as we all are in Pugwash – are always keen to support movements for freedom and justice. But the inherent fragility of a newly born state is frequently exploited by unscrupulous individuals or cliques seeking power for themselves, and setting up despotic regimes which give their people anything but freedom and justice. Until recently, there were hardly any democratically elected governments in the many states of the Third World.

But even if a newly independent state adopts a democratic system, its chances of establishing a secure and economically viable regime are very small. The fervour of patriotism that accompanies the attainment of independence usually leads the country to acquire all the trappings of sovereignty: an army and air force with all modern conventional weapons, a huge bureaucracy with embassies in every country, a national airline, and technologies, such as nuclear reactors (with perhaps the underlying thought that this may ultimately lead to the possession of nuclear weapons). All this costs money, and it usually leads to a heavy debt burden and economic ruin. Poverty, famine and disease are frequent adjuncts of independence.

In any case, the continuous division into many separate units flies in the face of the advances of science and technology, which have rendered the concept of the independent, sovereign nation-state obsolete. Just as in the past technological progress compelled the transition from fiefdom to the nation-state, so now the further technological advances dictate the replacement of the nation-state by a global entity.

In the distant past it was possible for small communities to exist separately, each self-sustained, and capable of providing the needs of its members with little dependence on, and communication with, other communities. Such insularity is now impossible even for very large nations. Modern means of transport and communication have made isolationism an obsolete notion. Thanks to the progress of science the world has become signally interdependent: anything happening in one part of the globe may have an effect in any other part. And the remarkable advances in communication have made it potentially possible for everybody to witness what is happening anywhere. Never in the history of civilization has the world community been so intimately interwoven.

Ironically, the same science that has done so much to raise the standard of living and to enrich our culture, has also provided powerful tools of destruction, even threatening to extinguish our civilization. Goods and information have become more accessible to all, but so have the means of killing; indeed, the most prosperous trade seems to be the trade in arms. Nations that cannot feed their people put priority on the acquisition of highly sophisticated armaments; missile technology is proliferating. Above all, there is the spectre of nuclear annihilation. The characteristic of this nuclear age is that for the first time in the history of mankind it has become possible for Man to destroy his own species.

Science has given a new meaning to interdependence: *if we do not learn to live together, we shall all perish together.*

From science we have received a warning to behave ourselves. And to science we should turn to provide the guidelines for proper behaviour. The main characteristics of science are universality and openness, and I believe that their adoption in the political arena will help to reduce incentives to war.

A major difference between the natural sciences and politics is that the former are governed by immutable laws of nature which have universal validity, whereas there has not been a corresponding principle to govern relations between nations. It is my thesis that such an overriding principle does now exist: it has emerged from the advances in the natural sciences, namely, the survival of mankind.

Survival of the species is the prime force in the living world. In the case of the human species, the high level of intellectual development extends this principle to the survival of civilization, because, as I have already remarked, progress in the natural sciences has created the potential for the destruction of civilization by man-made action. This new threat provides the motivation for the world community to organize itself in a way that would prevent such a catastrophe, as well as serving as the basis for a universal organizational structure.

If we start from this premise, it is obvious that the common interest in preserving civilization calls for a global approach to problems of security. This in turn calls on the inhabitants of all countries to recognize a new paramount duty to the world community: to accept a new loyalty, loyalty to mankind; to acquire a new citizenship, citizenship of the world.

At present, loyalty to one's nations is supreme: it overrides the loyalty to any subgroup, such as the family, local community or professional association, and it is enforced by national laws. These laws impose limitations on our freedom, but these limitations are generally accepted because of the recognition that this is the price paid for the protection provided by the state against outside enemies. Hitherto, the human species was not thought to need protection, because threats from natural causes, such as a collision with a large meteorite, were seen to have a very low probability. But now the threat comes from the inside, from the action of man: an abrupt end in a nuclear war, or slow extinction by poisoning the environment. Laws to protect us all are therefore urgently called for.

What I have attempted to show so far is that a radical change is needed if we are to reconcile the strivings of many entities for self-expression with the avoidance of war and preservation of our civilization. The radical change that I propose is the creation of a federal world government, with an international framework, which would include legislative power and a police force to ensure security to all its members; special organs would deal with requests for recognition by ethnic groups, etc, and protect the rights of minorities in any of its federal components.

Apart from stressing openness as a vital characteristic of the proposed system, I will not attempt at this stage a more detailed description of the structure of the World Government. I envisage it as a gradual evolution of the United Nations organization, with the steps of that evolution emerging from comprehensive studies. At this stage, the important point is to accept the concept, to recognize it as an idea whose time has come.

As I said earlier, both Einstein and Russell were strong proponents of World Government. In his "Open letter to the General Assembly of the United Nations" in 1947, Einstein said:

"As a matter of fact, the United Nations is an extremely important and useful institution provided the peoples and governments of the world realize that it is merely a transitional system toward the final goal, which is the establishment of a supranational authority vested with sufficient legislative and executive powers to keep the peace."

In his 1961 book *"Has Man a Future?"* Bertrand Russell goes into some detail about the need for, and structure of, a world government, which he saw as the only alternative to the self-destruction of the human race. He wrote:

"These technical advances, while they have made present international anarchy infinitely more dangerous than it used to be, have also made it techni- cally possible to establish a World Government which would be able to exert its power everywhere and could make armed resistance virtually impossible."

But, recognizing the realities of the time, he said:

"So long as the opposition between Communists and anti-Communists remains as fierce as it is at present, it will be difficult to win assent to any international institutions which might seem likely to impede the transition of individual nations from one camp to the other."

With the end of the titanic ideological struggle, the main obstacle to a World Government has been removed. Many steps have already been, and are being taken towards it. The United Nations, after many years in the doldrums has come back to play an important role in world security, and this role will be greatly strengthened when the recent proposals by Dr Boutros-Ghali are implemented. The time is propitious for starting the campaign for the next stage towards the goal of preventing war, to lay the foundation for a structure that will ensure lasting peace in the world.

A long and arduous task will confront those venturing to erect this structure. There is a substantial vested interest in fomenting conflicts among nations. Even among people of good will there will be strong opposition, particularly about giving up national sovereignty which is so deeply inculcated. Some will be worried that the World Government may not always be in benign hands. Others will be apprehensive of the vast bureaucracy this may entail. All these are valid concerns. But those who harbour such doubts, should consider the alternatives: think of the dangers inherent in the present division in the world; recall the many wars that have taken place since World War II with tens of millions of people killed in them; ponder on the present tragic situation in the Balkans which may be repeated scores of times; and meditate on the threat to all of us, should these conflicts escalate into a nuclear war.

Pugwash has achieved much in its attempts to reduce the nuclear danger, but we still have a long way to go before this danger is eliminated. We have an even longer way to go to eliminate all kinds of war, and the incentives to wage war. This is a daunting task, but let us not be too timid in setting our sights. Pugwash should be tall enough, to enable it to keep its feet firmly on the ground, yet the head high above the clouds with a clear vision of the future.

Let me conclude with a poem about such a vision. Tennyson wrote it exactly 150 years ago.

Men, my brothers, men the workers
ever reaping something new:
That which they have done but earnest
of the things that they shall do:
For I dipt into the future, far as
human eye could see,
Saw the Vision of the world, and all
the wonder that would be
Saw the heavens fill with commerce,
argosies of magic sails,
Pilots of the purple twilight, dropping
down with costly bales;
Heard the heavens fill with shouting,
and there rain'd a ghastly dew
From the nations' airy navies grappling
in the central blue;
For along the world-wide whisper
of the south-wind rushing warm,

With the standards of the peoples
plunging through the thunder-storms.
Till the war-drum throbb'd no longer
and the battle-flags were furl'd
In the Parliament of man,
the Federation of the World.

Appendix 6
Remember Your Humanity

Professor Joseph Rotblat
Founder and President, Pugwash Council
Nobel Lecture
10 December 1995, Oslo Norway

Your Majesties, Members of the Nobel Committee, Your Excellencies, Offices and Participants in the Pugwash Conferences, Ladies and Gentlemen:

At this momentous event in my life – the acceptance of the Nobel Peace Prize – I want to speak as a scientist, but also as a human being. From my earliest days I had a passion for science. But science, the exercise of the supreme power of the human intellect, was always linked in my mind with benefit to people. I saw science as being in harmony with humanity. I did not imagine that the second half of my life would be spent on efforts to avert a mortal danger to humanity created by science.

The practical release of nuclear energy was the outcome of many years of experimental and theoretical research. It had great potential for the common good. But the first the general public learned about this discovery was the news of the destruction of Hiroshima by the atom bomb. A splendid achievement of science and technology had turned malign. Science became identified with death and destruction.

It is painful to me to admit that this depiction of science was deserved. The decision to use the atom bomb on Japanese cities, and the consequent build up of enormous nuclear arsenals, was made by governments, on the basis of political and military perceptions. But scientists on both sides of the iron curtain played a very significant role in maintaining the momentum of the nuclear arms race throughout the four decades of the Cold War.

The role of scientists in the nuclear arms race was expressed bluntly by Lord Zuckerman, for many years Chief Scientific Adviser to the British Government:

When it comes to nuclear weapons . . . it is the man in the laboratory who at the start proposes that for this or that arcane reason it would be useful to improve an old or to devise a new nuclear warhead. It is he, the technician, not the commander in the field, who is at the heart of the arms race.

Long before the terrifying potential of the arms race was recognized, there was a widespread instinctive abhorrence of nuclear weapons, and a strong desire to get rid of them. Indeed, the very first resolution of the General Assembly of the United Nations – adopted unanimously – called for the elimination of nuclear weapons. But the world was then polarized by the bitter ideological struggle between East and West. There was no chance to meet this call. The chief task was to stop the arms race before it brought utter disaster. However, after the collapse of communism and the disintegration of the Soviet Union, any rationale for having nuclear weapons disappeared. The quest for their total elimination could be resumed. But the nuclear powers still cling tenaciously to their weapons.

Let me remind you that nuclear disarmament is not just an ardent desire of the people, as expressed in many resolutions of the United Nations. It is a legal commitment by the five official nuclear states, entered into when they signed the Non-Proliferation Treaty. Only a few months ago, when the indefinite extension of the Treaty was agreed, the nuclear powers committed themselves again to complete nuclear disarmament. This is still their declared goal. But the declarations are not matched by their policies, and this divergence seems to be intrinsic.

Since the end of the cold War the two main nuclear powers have begun to make big reductions in their nuclear arsenals. Each of them is dismantling about 2000 nuclear warheads a year. If this programme continued, all nuclear warheads could be dismantled in little over ten years from now. We have the technical means to create a nuclear-weapon-free world in about a decade. Alas, the present programme does not provide for this. When the START-2 treaty has been implemented – and remember it has not yet been ratified – we will be left with some 15,000 nuclear warheads, active and in reserve. Fifteen thousand weapons with an average yield of 20 Hiroshima bombs.

Unless there is a change in the basic philosophy, we will not see a reduction of nuclear arsenals to zero for a very long time, if ever. The present basic philosophy is nuclear deterrence. This was stated clearly in the US Nuclear Posture Review which concluded: *"Post-Cold War environment requires nuclear deterrence,"* and this is echoed by other nuclear states. Nuclear weapons are kept as a hedge against some unspecified dangers.

This policy is simply an inertial continuation from the Cold War era. The Cold War is over but Cold War thinking survives. Then, we were told that a world war was prevented by the existence of nuclear weapons. Now, we are told that nuclear weapons prevent all kinds of war. These are arguments that purport to prove a negative. I am reminded of a story told in my boyhood, at the time when radio communication began.

Two wise men were arguing about the ancient civilization in their respective countries. One said: 'my country has a long history of technological development: we have carried out deep excavations and found a wire, which shows that already in the old days we had the telegraph.' The other man retorted: 'we too made excavations; we dug much deeper than you and found . . . nothing, which proves that already in those days we had wireless communication!'

There is no direct evidence that nuclear weapons prevented a world war. Conversely, it is known that they nearly caused one. The most terrifying moment in my life was October 1962, during the Cuban Missile Crisis. I did not know all the facts – we have learned only recently how close we were to war – but I knew enough to make me tremble. The lives of millions of people were about to end abruptly; millions of others were to suffer a lingering death; much of our civilization was to be destroyed. It all hung on the decision of one man, Nikita Khrushchev: would he or would he not yield to the US ultimatum? This is the reality of nuclear weapons: they may trigger a world war; a war which, unlike previous ones, destroys all of civilization.

As for the assertion that nuclear weapons prevent wars, how many more wars are needed to refute this argument? Tens of millions have died in the many wars that have taken place since 1945. In a number of them nuclear states were directly involved. In two they were actually defeated. Having nuclear weapons was of no use to them.

To sum up, there is no evidence that a world without nuclear weapons would be a dangerous world. On the contrary, it would be a safer world, as I will show later.

We are told that the possession of nuclear weapons – in some cases even the testing of these weapons – is essential for national security. But this argument can be made by other countries as well. If the militarily most powerful – and least threatened – states need nuclear weapons for their security, how can one deny such security to countries that are truly insecure? The present nuclear policy is a recipe for proliferation. It is a policy for disaster.

To prevent this disaster – for the sake of humanity – we must get rid of all nuclear weapons.

Achieving this goal will take time, but it will never happen unless we make a start. Some essential steps towards it can be taken now. Several studies, and a number of public statements by senior military and political personalities, testify that – except for disputes between the present nuclear states – all military conflicts, as well as threats to peace, can be dealt with using conventional weapons. This means that the only function of nuclear weapons, while they exist, is to deter a nuclear attack. All nuclear weapon states should now recognize that this is so, and declare – in Treaty form – that they will never be the first to use nuclear weapons. This would open the way to the gradual, mutual reduction of nuclear arsenals, down to zero. It would also open the way for a Nuclear Weapons Convention. This would be universal – it would prohibit all possession of nuclear weapons.

We will need to work out the necessary verification system to safe-guard the Convention. A Pugwash study produced suggestions on these matters. The mechanisms for negotiating such a Convention already exist. Entering into negotiations does not commit the parties. There is no reason why they should not begin now. If not now, when?

So I ask the nuclear powers to abandon the out-of-date thinking of the Cold War period and take a fresh look. Above all, I appeal to them to bear in mind the long-term threat that nuclear weapons pose to humankind and to begin action towards their elimination. Remember your duty to humanity.

My second appeal is to my fellow scientists. I described earlier the disgraceful role played by a few scientists, caricatured as 'Dr

Strangeloves,' in fuelling the arms race. They did great damage to the image of science.

On the other side there are the scientists, in Pugwash and other bodies, who devote much of their time and ingenuity to averting the dangers created by advances in science and technology. However, they embrace only a small part of the scientific community. I want to address the scientific community as a whole.

You are doing fundamental work, pushing forward the frontiers of knowledge, but often you do it without giving much thought to the impact of your work on society. Precepts such as 'science is neutral' or 'science has nothing to do with politics,' still prevail. They are remnants of the ivory tower mentality, although the ivory tower was finally demolished by the Hiroshima bomb.

Here, for instance, is a question: Should any scientist work on the development of weapons of mass destruction? A clear "no" was the answer recently given by Hans Bethe. Professor Bethe, a Nobel Laureate, is the most senior of the surviving members of the Manhattan Project. On the occasion of the 50th Anniversary of Hiroshima, he issued a statement that I will quote in full.

As the Director of the Theoretical Division at Los Alamos, I participated at the most senior level in the World War II Manhattan Project that produced the first atomic weapons.

Now, at age 88, I am one of the few remaining such senior persons alive. Looking back at the half century since that time, I feel the most intense relief that these weapons have not been used since World War II, mixed with the horror that tens of thousands of such weapons have been built since that time — one hundred times more than any of us at Los Alamos could ever have imagined.

Today we are rightly in an era of disarmament and dismantlement of nuclear weapons. But in some countries nuclear weapons development still continues. Whether and when the various Nations of the World can agree to stop this is uncertain. But individual scientists can still influence this process by withholding their skills.

Accordingly, I call on all scientists in all countries to cease and desist from work creating, developing, improving and manufacturing further nuclear weapons — and, for that matter, other weapons of potential mass destruction such as chemical and biological weapons.

If all scientists heeded this call there would be no more new nuclear warheads; no French scientists at Mururoa; no new chemical and biological poisons. The arms race would be truly over.

But there are other areas of scientific research that may directly or indirectly lead to harm to society. This calls for constant vigilance. The purpose of some government or industrial research is sometimes concealed, and misleading information is presented to the public. It should be the duty of scientists to expose such malfeasance. "Whistle-blowing" should become part of the scientist's ethos. This may bring reprisals; a price to be paid for one's convictions. The price may be very heavy, as illustrated by the disproportionately severe punishment of Mordechai Vanunu. I believe he has suffered enough.

The time has come to formulate guidelines for the ethical conduct of scientists, perhaps in the form of a voluntary Hippocratic Oath. This would be particularly valuable for young scientists when they embark on a scientific career. The US Student Pugwash Group has taken up this idea – and that is very heartening.

At a time when science plays such a powerful role in the life of society, when the destiny of the whole of mankind may hinge on the results of scientific research, it is incumbent on all scientists to be fully conscious of that role, and conduct themselves accordingly. I appeal to my fellow scientists to remember their responsibility to humanity.

My third appeal is to my fellow citizens in all countries: Help us to establish lasting peace in the world.

I have to bring to your notice a terrifying reality: with the development of nuclear weapons Man has acquired, for the first time in history, the technical means to destroy the whole of civilization in a single act. Indeed, the whole human species is endangered, by nuclear weapons or by other means of wholesale destruction which further advances in science are likely to produce.

I have argued that we must eliminate nuclear weapons. While this would remove the immediate threat, it will not provide permanent security. Nuclear weapons cannot be disinvented. The knowledge of how to make them cannot be erased. Even in a nuclear-weapon-free world, should any of the great powers become involved in a military confrontation, they would be tempted to rebuild their nuclear arsenals. That would still be a better situation than the one we have now, because the

APPENDIXES |

rebuilding would take a considerable time, and in that time the dispute might be settled. A nuclear-weapon-free world would be safer than the present one. But the danger of the ultimate catastrophe would still be there.

The only way to prevent it is to abolish war altogether. War must cease to be an admissible social institution. We must learn to resolve our disputes by means other than military confrontation.

This need was recognized forty years ago when we said in the *Russell–Einstein Manifesto*:

Here then is the problem which we present to you, stark and dreadful, and inescapable: shall we put an end to the human race: or shall mankind renounce war?

The abolition of war is also the commitment of the nuclear weapon states: Article VI of the NPT calls for a treaty on general and complete disarmament under strict and effective international control.

Any international treaty entails some surrender of national sovereignty, and is generally unpopular. As we said in the Russell–Einstein Manifesto: *"The abolition of war will demand distasteful limitations of national sovereignty."* Whatever system of governance is eventually adopted, it is important that it carries the people with it. We need to convey the message that safeguarding our common property, humankind, will require developing in each of us a new loyalty: a loyalty to mankind. It calls for the nurturing of a feeling of belonging to the human race. We have to become world citizens.

Notwithstanding the fragmentation that has occurred since the end of the cold War, and the many wars for recognition of national or ethnic identities, I believe that the prospects for the acceptance of this new loyalty are now better than at the time of the Russell–Einstein Manifesto. This is so largely because of the enormous progress made by science and technology during these 40 years. The fantastic advances in communication and transportation have shrunk our globe. All nations of the world have become close neighbours. Modern information techniques enable us to learn instantly about every event in every part of the globe. We can talk to each other via the various networks. This facility will improve enormously with time, because the achievements so far have only scratched the surface. Technology is driving us together. In many ways we are becoming like one family. In advocating the new loyalty to mankind I am not suggesting that we give up national loyalties. Each of us has loyalties to several groups – from the smallest, the family, to the largest, at present, the nation. Many of these groups provide protection for their members. With the global threats resulting from science and technology, the whole of humankind now needs protection. We have to extend our loyalty to the whole of the human race.

What we are advocating in Pugwash, a war-free world, will be seen by many as a Utopian dream. It is not Utopian. There already exist in the world large regions, for example, the European Union, within which war is inconceivable. What is needed is to extend these to cover the world's major powers.

In any case, we have no choice. The alternative is unacceptable. Let me quote the last passage of the *Russell–Einstein Manifesto*:

We appeal, as human beings, to human beings: Remember your humanity and forget the rest. If you can do so, the way lies open for a new paradise; if you cannot, there lies before you the risk of universal death.

The quest for a war-free world has a basic purpose: survival. But if in the process we learn how to achieve it by love rather than by fear, by kindness rather than by compulsion; if in the process we learn to combine the essential with the enjoyable, the expedient with the benevolent, the practical with the beautiful, this will be an extra incentive to embark on this great task.

Above all, remember your humanity.

Appendix 7

53rd Pugwash Conference on Science and World Affairs Advancing Human Security: The Role of Technology and Politics

Halifax and Pugwash, Nova Scotia, Canada, 17–21 July, 2003

Public Forum
Friday, July 18, 2003
Ondaatje Auditorium, Dalhousie University, Halifax

The Nuclear Issue: Pugwash and the Bush Policies
by Sir Joseph Rotblat*
President Emeritus, Pugwash Conferences

For excerpts of Prof. Joseph Rotblat's speech in the international media, please see the following:

The Sunday News (Karachi, Pakistan): www.jang.com.pk/thenews/
    aug2003-weekly/nos-10-08-2003/pol1.htm#8
Aftenposten (Oslo, Norway):www.aftenposten.no/meninger/kronikker
    /article.jhtml?articleID=597864

This paper is mainly concerned with the nuclear issue, specifically with the dangers to the world that may arise from the nuclear policies of the George W. Bush Administration. But in order to put these policies into a proper perspective, I have to start with observations on the general doctrines and strategies of this Administration.

I should declare, from the start, that I am strongly critical of the present US Administration in its conduct of world affairs. In the highly charged political climate of the recent months – largely related to the Iraq debacle – anyone criticizing the Bush Administration has immediately been branded as anti-American, and placed in the defensive position of having to begin with a statement that one is not anti-American.

So let me say this clearly: I am not anti-American. On the contrary, I submit that it is the policies of the current Administration that should be called anti-American, because – in my opinion – they do no represent the views of the majority of the American people. I am convinced that these policies would not have been pursued if Al Gore had won the election in 2000. You will remember that – even with the distraction of Ralph Nader – Al Gore had a majority in the national vote, and it was only through some questionable manoevres that he was deprived of the Presidency. It seems to me very unlikely that, had he been elected, Al Gore would have alienated so many to such an extent.

It is important to note that the current polarization of the world is largely the consequence of the Bush slogan: "*You are either with us or against us*". This was initially applied to the campaign against al-Qaeda, but it puts all those who do not fully agree with the Bush policies into the category of villains. There are many, perhaps a majority in the world, who are strongly against terrorists, and ready to join in actions against them, but are not happy with the Bush policies. These policies are seen by many outside the United States as aiming at establishing a US hegemony in the world, and treating international undertakings with contempt, to be adhered to only if they suit the interest of the United States.

What I find so repugnant about these policies is their blatant hypocrisy. The USA proclaims itself as the champion of democracy in the world, while actually imposing its will in a dictatorial manner. It is supposed to uphold the rules of law, yet violates legal commitments under international treaties. It castigates members of the United Nations for exercising their rights under existing rules but takes military action against a member state without the authority of the United Nations.

A central criticism of the United Nations made by the Bush team is that it is ineffective, a useless and enfeebled organ, incapable of taking decisive action. This sort of criticism has traditionally been leveled at democracies by totalitarian regimes. Long discussions and protracted negotiations are an inherent feature of a democratic system, in which the needs and aspirations of many groups or nations have to be reconciled in a peaceful manner. The Bush Administration has no truck with such approaches, even though it professes to champion democracy.

In my view, such policies are unacceptable in a civilized society because in the long run, they would spell the ruin of civilization.

The pursuit of these policies was evident in the campaign against Iraq. The stated justification was to disarm Iraq of weapons of mass destruction, but others see it primarily as an attempt to increase the US influence in the Middle East. There is plenty of documentary evidence to support the thesis that the main reason for bringing down the Saddam Hussein regime in Iraq – and making similar threats against Syria and Iran – was to change the political configuration in the Middle East so as to give the United States political, economic and military control of that region.

The history of these endeavours, is now general knowledge, but I want to recall some salient points.

Even during the Cold War years, various right wing groups in the United States – who have become known as neo-conservatives – advocated strong aggressive foreign policies. These groups had considerable sway during the Reagan Presidency, but is was after the end of the Cold War – and the outcome of the first Gulf War, which they saw as having left the business unfinished – that they became really active. In the spring of 1992 a document was produced, called *Defense Policy Guidance*, which was stunning in the clarity and ambition of its vision of a new US foreign and military policy. It called for US dominance by preventing the rise of any potentially hostile power, and for a policy of pre-emptive military action against states suspected of developing weapons of mass destruction. The document was written by two relatively unknown functionaries in the Pentagon's policy department. They were Paul Wolfowitz and Lewis Libby; their boss at the time was Dick Cheney, then Secretary for Defense. All three are now prominent members of the Bush Administration.

In July 1996, the Institute for Advanced Strategic and Political Studies issued a document entitled *"A Clean Break: a New Strategy for Securing the Realm"*. The head of the Institute was Richard Perle – for years known as the Prince of Darkness, for his extreme views, and strong support of the Israel lobby. The document called on the then Israeli Prime Minister, Benjamin Netanyahu, to adopt a radical change in policy, starting with a repudiation of the Oslo Accords, and to be followed by a campaign to eliminate Saddam Hussein and destabilize the governments of Syria, Lebanon, Saudi Arabia, and Iran.

In February 1998, Richard Perle wrote an Open Letter to President Clinton, demanding a full-scale drive for a regime change in Baghdad. It had 25 signatories, including many who are now in the Bush Administration, e.g.: Donald Rumsfeld—now Defense Secretary, and Paul Wolfowitz – now Deputy Defense Secretary.

The al-Qaeda attack of September 11 provided the opportunity for these policies to be put into practice. The case for a *Pax Americana* had been set out, and its first stage was implemented in the war against Iraq.

The prolonged squabbles over UN Resolutions and inspections, aiming at giving legitimacy to the war, seem to have been just a charade, intended to create the impression that it was not the USA alone but a coalition that was involved in the anti-Iraq campaign. The decision to overthrow the Saddam Hussein regime having been taken much earlier, it was only the time for its implementation that had to be chosen. This was probably dictated not by the outcome of the Hans Blix inspections, but by the need to assemble the necessary military strength.

The military strength of the USA is truly awesome. Since the end of the Cold War, the Americans have built up an enormous military potential. Making use of the latest advances in science and the achievements in technology – and supported by budgets of astronomical dimensions – the United States has become the greatest military power that ever existed; nearly exceeding in sophistication all other nations combined. Against this might, the Iraqi army, with antiquated tanks and no air-power to provide cover, did not stand a chance.

Of course, the fact that Saddam Hussein's regime was rotten, and was kept from falling apart entirely by the terror imposed by a small number of thugs, contributed to its rapid demise. The claim by Rumsfeld *et al.* that Iraq posed a threat to other nations, including the United States, was just laughable.

Indeed, the official reason for the military attack on Iraq – the removal of weapons of mass destruction – has proven to be completely indefensible, since no such weapons have so far been found, despite the intense search carried out by large groups of experts appointed by the USA. As time goes on, and the WMDs are not found, there will be an attempt to play down the importance of finding them, but this will not alter the fact that the war was started on false premises.

All the same, it would be hypocritical for those of us who were against the war not to rejoice over the downfall of a tyrannical regime, and not to admit that this would not have come about so quickly without military intervention. But the price we paid for this is far too high: it has reinstated in world affairs the old maxim that the *ends justify the means*.

The events of the recent months are a severe setback to those who believe that morality and adherence to the rules of law should be our guiding principles. For the time being, the rule seems to be: *might is right*, and in submitting to this rule, the governments of many countries may be driven to adopt a pragmatic policy; they may be forced to acknowledge that there is now a single superpower; they may feel obliged to accept the role of the United States as the world's policeman.

But this cannot be a permanent solution. Even if the Americans were less arrogant in pursuing that role than they are now, a system with a built-in inequality is bound to be unstable. It is bound to create resentment, a resentment that will find expression in various ways, including an increase in international terrorism. This in turn will force the "policemen" to take countermeasures, which will make the inequality even more acute. Democracy in the world, as we know it today, would be ended.

This is a possible scenario, but it need not happen. My main hope is that the opposition to it will come from within the United States itself. At present, Bush is very popular and carries a majority of public opinion: this is the usual wave of patriotism which comes with a military victory, but it is already decreasing significantly. I believe that the strong anti-war demonstrations that we saw earlier are a true reflection of the views of the majority of the American people. Somehow, I do not see the American people accepting the role assigned to them by the clique that has hijacked the Administration. Public opinion is bound to turn when the dangers associated with the current policies become apparent. My main worry is that in the meantime these dangers may lead to catastrophic results. The greatest dangers derive from the nuclear doctrines pursued by the Bush Administration.

These new doctrines have been comprehensively analysed by Steven Miller in a paper, "Skepticism Triumphant", an updated version of a presentation he made at the Pugwash conference in Agra last year. He contrasts the views of the "Skeptics", by which he means the Bush Administration, against those of the arms controllers. His conclusion is that *arms control is dead*.

This conclusion is probably correct, but is does not follow from this that we have to accept fatalistically the new doctrines. Arms control and unilateral policies are not the only options. In his paper, Steven Miller was mainly concerned with contrasting these two, and therefore he left out from consideration another alternative to arms control, namely, nuclear disarmament. In Pugwash we faced, from the beginning, the dilemma of the two approaches: arms control versus disarmament. A few years ago we spent much time, in the Council and in special workshops, discussing the pros and cons of the two approaches.

This dispute has now been brought to an end by the entry onto the scene of the new approach. Arms control is now dead. But, as discussed earlier, the policy of the Bush Administration, envisaging US world dominance, is unacceptable. I submit that this leaves only one option for Pugwash: to pursue nuclear disarmament.

The elimination of nuclear weapons has always been the goal of Pugwash, following the call in the Russell–Einstein Manifesto. We have pursued this goal for moral reasons, because ethical issues have always played a major role in Pugwash: any use of nuclear weapons has been seen as immoral. But we have also seen in our goals a basic purpose: survival. Any use of nuclear weapons would carry the danger of escalation and a threat to our continued existence.

But the use of nuclear weapons is explicitly contemplated in the policies of the Bush Administration.

These policies have been promulgated in a number of statements, most of them made during the last year. The following documents are of particular importance:

- Nuclear Posture Review. January, 2002
- The National Security Strategy of the United States of America. September, 2002
- National Strategy to Combat Weapons of Mass Destruction. December 2002

- National Policy on Ballistic Missile Defense. May 2003

These policies seem to have two aims: one, a defensive strategy to make the USA invulnerable to an attack from outside; the second, an offensive strategy, to threaten an unfriendly regime with military action, including the use of nuclear weapons, if it attempts to acquire WMDs for itself.

For the first purpose, the decision was made to give a high priority to missile defence. As a first step, the USA abrogated the Anti-Ballistic Missile Treaty, which had been previously considered the bedrock of the arms control system. A hugely increased budget has been provided for a missile defence project, which is said to be essential in a world of potential threats from weapons of mass destruction.

But it is in the offensive aspect that the biggest changes have occurred. The new Nuclear Posture Review spells out a strategy which incorporates nuclear capability into conventional war planning. The previous doctrine of deterrence, by which the actual use of nuclear weapons was seen as a last resort, when everything else had failed, has been thrown overboard. In the new doctrine, nuclear weapons have become a standard part of military strategy; they would be used in a conflict just like any other explosives. This represents a major shift in the whole rationale for nuclear weapons.

The main reason for this change seems to be the fear that states seen as unfriendly to the USA may acquire weapons of mass destruction: *"We will not permit the world's most dangerous regimes and terrorists to threaten us with the world's most destructive weapons."*

In this pursuit, the Bush Administration is prepared to go very far, including pre-emptive strikes: *"We must be prepared to stop rogue states and their terrorist clients before they are able to threaten or use weapons of mass destruction against the United States and our allies and friends."* And it goes on: *"To forestall or prevent such hostile acts by our adversaries, the United States will, if necessary, act pre-emptively."*

The implementation of this policy has already begun. The United States is designing a new nuclear warhead of low yield, but with a shape that would give it a very high penetrating power into concrete, the *"robust nuclear earth penetrator"*. It is intended to destroy bunkers with thick concrete walls in which weapons of mass destruction may be stored, or enemy leaders may seek shelter.

To enable this project to go ahead the US Senate has already decided to rescind the long-standing prohibition on the development of low yield nuclear weapons. Other types of warheads are also contemplated.

The new weapons will have to be tested. At present there is a treaty prohibiting the testing of nuclear weapons (except in sub-critical assemblies), the Comprehensive Test Ban Treaty, which the United States has signed but not ratified. Given the contempt of the Bush Administration for international treaties, little excuse would be needed to authorize the testing of the new weapon. Indeed, the need to resume testing is now openly advocated.

If the USA resumed testing, this would be a signal to other nuclear weapon states to do the same. China would be almost certain to resume testing. After the US decision to develop ballistic missile defences, China feels vulnerable, and is likely to attempt to reduce its vulnerability by modernizing and enlarging its nuclear arsenal. An opinion is building up that: *"China should realize that the present minimum nuclear arsenal is inadequate to meet the new challenges, and therefore should greatly expand its nuclear force to the extent that it can be actually used in different scenarios."* At present this is a minority view, but it may become significant should the USA resume testing. Other states with nuclear weapons, such as India or Pakistan, might use the window of opportunity opened by the USA to update their arsenals. The danger of a new nuclear arms race is real.

Another worry about the development of the new bomb is that it would blur the distinction between nuclear and conventional weapons. The chief characteristic of a nuclear weapon is its enormous destructive power, unique even in comparison with current chemical or biological weaponry, also designated as weapons of mass destruction. This has resulted in a taboo on the use of nuclear weapons in combat, a taboo that has held out since Nagasaki. But if at one end of the spectrum a nuclear bomb can be manufactured which does not differ quantitatively from ordinary explosives, then the qualitative difference will also disappear; the nuclear threshold will be crossed, and nuclear weapons will gradually come to be seen as a tool of war, even though the danger they present to the existence of the human race will remain.

For the USA, the distinction between nuclear and conventional weapons has already been eroded, as was made clear in the Nuclear

Posture Review, but the situation has become even more threatening with the additional disposition to act pre-emptively.

The danger of this policy can hardly be over-emphasized. If the militarily mightiest country declares its readiness to carry out a pre-emptive use of nuclear weapons, others may soon follow. The Kashmir crisis, in May last year, is a stark warning of the reality of the nuclear peril.

India's declared policy is not to be the first to use nuclear weapons. But if the United States-whose nuclear policies are largely followed by India-makes a pre-emptive nuclear use part of its doctrine, this would give India the legitimacy to similarly threaten pre-emptive action against Pakistan. George Fernandes, India's Minister for Defence, said recently: India had *a much better case to go for pre-emptive action against Pakistan than the United States has in Iraq.* More likely perhaps is that Pakistan would carry this out first.

Taiwan presents another potential scenario for a pre-emptive nuclear strike by the United States. Should the Taiwan authorities decide to declare independence, this would inevitably result in an attempted military invasion by mainland China. The USA, which is committed to the defence of Taiwan, may then opt for a pre-emptive strike.

And we still have the problem of North Korea, described by Bush as one of the "axis of evil". Under the Bush dictum not to allow the possession of weapons of mass destruction by any state considered to be hostile, North Korea will be called upon to close down all work on nuclear weapons. It is by no means certain that Kim Jong Il will submit to these demands, and a critical situation may arise in that part of the world.

A major worry in this respect are developments in Japan. So far Japan has been kept out of the nuclear weapons club by Article 9 of its constitution:

" . . . *the Japanese people forever renounce . . . the threat or use of force as means of settling international disputes.*"

However, partly at the urging of the USA, strong tendencies are now appearing-with the backing of the Prime Minister, Junichiro Koizumi-to revise the constitution so as to make it legal for Japan to become a nuclear-weapon state.

Altogether, the aggressive policy of the United States, under the Bush Administration, has created a precarious situation in world affairs, with a greatly increased danger of nuclear weapons being used in combat.

Moreover, if the use of nuclear weapons is made legal, it would preclude passing of laws to prevent the development of new types of weapons, with even greater destructive potential than current WMDs- a truly horrifying prospect. Sir Martin Rees, the British Astronomer Royal, gives civilization a 50/50 chance of surviving this century. Others believe that this is optimistic.

What should be the Pugwash stand on this matter? Does the new situation call for a corresponding change in our activities?

Let me first state that I fully support the efforts made by the Secretary-General towards the resolution of local conflicts, particularly in the Middle East. His success in bringing together personalities from opposing camps encourages us to continue these activities; they may prevent a regional crisis from getting out of control.

But it is the central issue that I am concerned about. A year ago, in La Jolla, we have adopted the Goals of Pugwash for the next five years. The relevant document states: "*Pugwash is strongly committed to the goal of abolishing all nuclear weapons. It is imperative that Pugwash constantly remind the international community of the immorality, illegality, and peril inherent in nuclear weapons, and to propose concrete steps towards their elimination.*" In the second year of the Quinquennium it is high time to take these steps.

Any attempt to achieve our goals by persuading the Bush Administration to change its policies through logical persuasion, or by appealing to moral instincts, would be hopeless and a complete waste of time. But it may not be a waste of time if such an appeal is made to the general public. As I said earlier, hope lies in a change of public opinion, particularly in the United States, to rise in opposition to the current poli- cies, and throw them out in the process usually employed in democratic countries, namely, in free elections. Therefore, my suggestion is that the Pugwash effort should be towards an acceleration of that process in a campaign to influence public opinion, a campaign based on principles of morality and equity.

The immorality in the use of nuclear weapons is taken for granted, but this aspect is very seldom raised when calling for nuclear disarma- ment. We are told that a campaign based on moral principles is a non-starter, and we are afraid of appearing naïve, and divorced from reality. I see in the use of this argument evidence that we have allowed ethical considerations to be ignored for far too long. We are accused of not being realistic, when what we are trying to do is to prevent real dangers, the dangers that would result from the current policies of the Bush Administration.

The public at large is ignorant about these dangers and we urgently need a campaign of public education.

The other basic principle is adherence to international law. It is a sine qua non of a civilized society that nations fulfil their legal obligations and respect international law. World peace cannot be achieved without adherence to international treaties.

There is much deliberate obfuscation and brainwashing in this respect. Let me illustrate this with the example which happens to be at the heart of the problem, the problem of the Non-Proliferation Treaty (NPT).

Pugwash was very much involved in this treaty, in its earliest years, when we saw it as an important measure towards the elimination of nuclear weapons. Let me recall the salient facts about the NPT, to which 98 percent of nations have subscribed. In accordance with the treaty, all non-nuclear states that signed it undertook not to acquire nuclear weapons in any way. At the same time, the five states which officially possessed those weapons-by virtue of the fact that they had tested them by a certain date-undertook to get rid of theirs. The relevant Article VI reads:

"Each of the Parties to the Treaty undertakes to pursue negotiations in good faith on effective measures relating to cessation of the nuclear arms race at an early date and to nuclear disarmament, and on a treaty on general and complete disarmament under strict and effective international control."

By signing and ratifying the NPT, the nuclear member states are legally committed to nuclear disarmament. The hawks in those states, in an attempt to retain nuclear weapons, utilized an ambiguity in Article VI, which makes it appear that nuclear disarmament is linked with the achievement of general and complete disarmament. But the NPT Review Conference-an official part of the implementation of the NPT-at its session in 2000, removed this ambiguity in a statement issued by all five nuclear weapons states. It contains the following:

" . . . an unequivocal undertaking by the nuclear-weapon states to accomplish the total elimination of their nuclear arsenals leading to nuclear disarmament to which all States Parties are committed under Article VI."

This makes the situation perfectly clear. The Bush policy, which is based on the continued existence (and use) of nuclear weapons, is in direct contradiction to the legally binding NPT.

But the Bush Administration seems to have managed to convince the public that only a part of the NPT, the part that applies to the non-nuclear states, is valid, and that therefore states which violate it-as Iran now stands accused of doing-must be punished for the transgression. The part concerning the obligation of the nuclear states is deliberately being obliterated. Let me cite two items which recently appeared in British national newspapers:

"At a meeting of the IAEA today, the US will urge it to declare Tehran in breach of the Nuclear Non-Proliferation Treaty. **The treaty seeks to confine nuclear weapons to Russia, Britain, France, China and America."**

I have emphasized the second sentence because it displays the complete reversal of the purpose of the NPT.

The other newspaper – none other than *The Times* – reports similarly:

"It {the NPT} was established to stop the spread of nuclear weapons beyond the original declared nuclear powers of the US, China, Russia, the UK and France."

There is no mention of the obligation of the latter.

We are being told all the time how dangerous nuclear weapons are and that they must not be allowed to fall into the hands of undesirable elements or rogue regimes:

"Weapons of mass destruction . . . nuclear, biological, and chemical – in the possession of hostile states and terrorists, represent one of the greatest security challenges facing the United States."

What we are not being told is that these weapons are just as dangerous in the possession of friendly nations. We are not being reminded that – with the realization of these dangers – even the United

States has undertaken to get rid of its own nuclear arsenal. We are facing here a basic issue in which the ethical and legal aspects are intertwined. The use of nuclear weapons is seen by the great majority of people in the world as immoral, due to their indiscriminate nature and unprecedented destructive power. Their possession — and therefore likely use — is thus equally unacceptable, whether by "rogue" or benevolent regimes.

The elimination of nuclear weapons has been the declared aim of the United Nations from the beginning, and resolutions to this effect are passed, year after year, by large majorities of the General Assembly. These resolutions are ignored by the nuclear weapon states, as are all attempts to discuss the issue by the organ set up for this purpose, the Conference on Disarmament in Geneva.

There is a need to keep hammering home the point that America's stand on the NPT issue is iniquitous. It has signed and ratified an international treaty which commits it to get rid of nuclear weapons, yet it is pursuing a policy which demands the indefinite retention of these weapons.

We have to keep on highlighting the fundamental inconsistency in the US policies. The USA must make a choice: if it wants to keep nuclear weapons, then it should withdraw from the NPT (which would probably result in a massive increase in the number of nuclear weapon states). Otherwise, it must abide by the terms of the NPT and get rid of its nuclear arsenals. Tertium non datur. There is no third way.

I believe that a campaign to educate and influence public opinion, centered on the issue of the NPT, would stand a good chance of being successful.

The task of influencing public opinion is far too big for an organization like Pugwash to undertake by itself. Collaboration with other organizations would be essential. This would go against our traditional *modus vivendi*; Puwash has often been accused — perhaps justifiably — of being an exclusive club. But even if our mode of work has been justified in the past, I believe that the time has come to open up. I am not advocating that Pugwash should become a mass movement; what I am suggesting is that we should be more willing to collaborate with other organizations in the sense of spearheading a large effort to provide information to the general public. Pugwash is a movement of scientists, but the job of the scientist is not only to do original research; education is an essential element of it. And this is in essence what I propose.

An initiative in this direction has already been started by the British Pugwash Group. In setting up a *"Nuclear Weapons Awareness Project"*, the British Pugwash Group is collaborating with about a dozen other British organizations, ranging from BASIC (the British American Security Information Council) to MEDACT (Medical Action), from CND to Greenpeace. An account of this Project is presented by John Finney in paper submitted to this Conference. I suggest that the Pugwash Council should take it up and find ways to implement it on an international scale.

Let me now conclude with some simple observations of a more general nature, but relevant to the problems I have raised in this paper.

I believe in the inherent goodness of Man. What would be the point of keeping the human species if this were not true! But then our task must be to ensure that this belief gains general acceptance.

We still conduct world affairs on the outdated principle that our survival demands being militarily strong. This is a remnant of our early history, when Man had to resort to violence in order to survive or to ensure continuation of the species. It completely ignores the radical changes that have occurred as a result of the advances in science and technology, changes which make such a stand no longer necessary. If equitably distributed, our resources could be sufficient to meet the basic needs of the world population, despite its huge increase.

Moreover, thanks largely to the fantastic progress in technology, our world is becoming more and more interdependent, more and more transparent, more and more interactive. Inherent in these developments is a set of agreements, ranging from confidence-building measures to formal international treaties; from protection of the environment to the clearance of mine fields; from Interpol to the International Criminal Court; from ensuring intellectual property rights to the Declaration of Human Rights. Respect for, and strict adherence to, the terms of international agreements are at the basis of a civilized society. Without this, anarchy and terrorism would reign, the very perils President Bush is allegedly committed to eradicate. While he intends to tackle this issue by military means, we must strive to achieve it by peaceful means. While the Bush Administration plans to act unilaterally, we have to ensure that world security is entrusted to the United Nations, the institution set up for this purpose. And we must link our respect for the law with strong moral principles.

Many of you are professional people, trained to look at problems in a detached, realistic, non-sentimental approach. But we are all, primarily, human beings, anxious to provide security for our nearest and dearest, and peace for fellow citizens of our nation and the world. We want to see a world in which relations between people and between nations are based on compassion, not greed; on generosity, not jealousy; on persuasion, not force; on equity, not oppression.

These are simple, some will say romantic, sentiments, but they are also realistic necessities. In a world armed with weapons of mass destruction, the use of which might bring the whole of civilization to an end, we cannot afford a polarized community, with its inherent threat of military confrontations. In this technological age, a global, equitable community, to which we all belong as world citizens, has become a vital necessity.

Sir Joseph Rotblat is co-recipient, with the Pugwash Conferences, of the 1995 Nobel Peace Prize. A signatory of the Russell–Einstein Manifesto in 1955 and one of the founders of the Pugwash Conferences, he attended the first meeting in Pugwash, Nova Scotia in July 1957, and later served as the organization's President.

For more information, please contact Dr. Jeffrey Boutwell, Executive Director, Pugwash Conferences, in Washington, DC at 1-202-478-3440, or pugwashdc@aol.com

* The views expressed are those of the author, and not of the Pugwash Council or Pugwash Conferences.

Sources

Audio sources

In my attempts to understand Joseph Rotblat, I have made extensive use of the interviews stored in the British Library Sound Archive (BLSA) (call number F7208 and onwards). The archive comprises some 21 audio tapes and constitutes a series of interviews given to Katherine Thompson in Rotblat's own home. The interviews themselves took place between 1999 (May) and 2002. They represent an invaluable resource, which (to my knowledge) has not been used in the literature on Rotblat. Transcripts are not available. I have used these recordings as an essential guide to Rotblat's achievements, life and work – and also to understanding some of the literature on him.

The National Security Archive–Cold War Interviews (November 15, 1998, Episode 8, SPUTNIK) have also been very useful. These belong to a non-governmental, non-profit organization of scientists and journalists who provided a 'home' for formerly secret US government information obtained under The Freedom of Information Act. Full transcripts are available on the internet, from the National Security Archive of Cold War Interviews, at

www.gwu.edu/~nsarchiv/coldwar/interviews (last accessed 19 January 2009).

Published sources

Primary

J. Rotblat, 1941. 'Application of the coincidence method for the measurement of short-lived periods', *Proceedings of the Royal Society*, A 177: 260–71.

J. Rotblat, 1943. 'Neutrons from spontaneous fission', British Report (BR 241).

J. Rotblat, 1949. 'Some applications of radioactive tracers in medicine', *British Scientific News*, 2.19: 201–4.

J. Rotblat, 1955. 'The 15 MeV linear accelerator at St Bartholomew's Hospital', *Nature*, 175: 745–7.

J. Rotblat, 1967. *PUGWASH: The First Ten Years*, Humanities Press.

G. Ansell and J. Rotblat, 1948. 'Radioactive iodine as a diagnostic aid for intrathoracic goitre', *British Journal of Radiation*, 21: 552–8.

R. Hinde and J. Rotblat, 2003. *War No More*, Pluto Books.

P. J. Lindop and J. Rotblat, 1961. 'Shortening of life and causes of death in mice exposed to a single whole-body dose of radiation', *Nature*, 189: 645–8.

P. J. Lindop and J. Rotblat, 1965. 'Life-shortening in mice exposed to radiation: Effects of age and hypoxia', *Nature*, 208, 1070–2.

Secondary

C. D. King, 1997. Sir James Chadwick and his medical plans for then 37-inch cyclotron', *Medical Historian, The Bulletin of Liverpool Medical History Society*, 9, pp. 43–55.

L. Badash, 1995. *Scientists and the Development of Nuclear Weapons*, Humanity Books.

R. Braun, R. Hinde, D. Krieger, H. Kroto and S. Milne (eds), 2007. *Joseph Rotblat: Visionary for Peace*, Wiley–Vich.

J. Chadwick, 1938. 'The cyclotron and its applications', *Nature*, 142: 630–4.

J. Chadwick, 1947. 'Atomic energy', *Lancet*, 252, 1: 315–20.

J. Chadwick to J. Cockcroft, in 'Cockcroft's Papers 20/5' (8.1.1940), Churchill Archives Centre, Churchill College, Cambridge; reproduced in A. Brown, 1997, *The Neutron and the Bomb*, Oxford University Press.

J. Cox, 1981. *Overkill: The Story of Modern Weapons*, Penguin.

O. Frisch, 1979. *What Little I Remember*, Cambridge University Press.

P. Rowlands and V. Attwood (eds), 2006. *War and Peace. The Life and Work of Joseph Rotblat*, Liverpool University Press.

M. Underwood, 2008. 'Joseph Rotblat: Influences, scientific achievements and legacy', *Physics Education*, 43: 604–12.

M. Underwood, 'Joseph Rotblat: The conscience of this nuclear age', *Nuclear Age Peace Foundation Issue*, 136 (October 2008), www.wagingpeace. org/ articles/2008/10/28.

M. Underwood, 'Joseph Rotblat and the moral responsibilities of the scientist', 'Science and Engineering Ethics' (2009, in press).

Index